GW00659862

MAKING
SHIPS IN BOTTLES

BEGINNERS TO ADVANCED
"Towards easier and better modelling"

MAKING SHIPS IN BOTTLES

BEGINNERS TO ADVANCED

"Towards easier and better modelling"

LÉON LABISTOUR

MARINE ARTS PUBLICATIONS

Copyright © Léon Labistour 1990
All Rights Reserved.

Except for use in a review, no part of this publication may be reproduced,
stored in a retrieval system, or transmitted in any form or by any means,
without prior permission of the publisher.

First published 1990 by Marine Arts Publications,
"Seascape",
Robin Hood's Bay,
Whitby, North Yorkshire,
England. YO22 4SH.

ISBN 0-9516184-0-7
Making Ships in Bottles

Design and page planning by
Graham Boddy

Front cover design by
Pat Labistour

Colour photography by
Bill Croke, Whitby.

Reproduction by City Ensign Ltd.
Maritime House,
Omega Business Park,
Hull HU3 2BP.

Typeset in Palatino by
Phototype Print Services,
St. Andrew's Quay,
Hull HU3 4PP.

Printed and bound by
Ryedale Printing Works Ltd.,
Kirbymoorside,
York YO6 6DN.

To Pat,

my 1st class First Mate

CONTENTS

FOREWORD

ACKNOWLEDGEMENTS

INTRODUCTION

List of photographs

List of plans

List of drawings

FOREWORD

To consider introducing a new text book, the subject of which is already well covered by established literature, must give any intending Author great initial pause.

There was no exception in my case and the very thought of putting pen to paper only came seriously to mind following an in-depth perusal of the many treatises on Ship Bottling, some dating back almost half a century. Excellent though many of these were, I realised (not without some surprise) that 35 years of day-by-day ship modelling had provided me with much to offer in the way of new and different method and technique. This fact, it was clear, could be related directly to a constant striving, over the years, to maintain within the family craft business, a particular activity which always contributed great pleasure and interest.

Financial viability being of prime consideration, constant review of all working routines was of paramount importance. Methods and technique of optimum efficiency evolved and at first, it was quite astounding to discover how one had laboured unnecessarily! Profit motives apart, however, I think it behoves any hobbyist to pursue his craft with studied efficacy which, in turn, invariably leads to better results. Thus, the sub-title of my book was created!

Further to the idea – omission of technical terms, where possible, has been given consideration and I have concentrated on the main purpose of moving towards the end product. Those who wish, can make reference to a whole host of books to become acquainted with every yard, line and spar on a sailing ship.

My earnest hope is that this modest book will sufficiently inspire anyone seeking a really satisfying hobby, which, basic principles and skills once learnt, leads on to modelling where complete individuality is allowed to assert itself.

Léon Labistour,
"Seascape",
Robin Hood's Bay,
North Yorkshire,
England.

ACKNOWLEDGEMENTS

Throughout the creation of my book, it has been a constant source of amazement that I have had immediate access to the services of a willing, enthusiastic and skilled supportive 'crew'. To these, I tender my grateful thanks:

A text book of this nature relies to a great extent on illustrations that give clear support to the text and Colin Harrison's professional touch to all my working plans, along with his excellent isometric and other drawings, helps steer the modeller on my intended course – 'towards easier and better modelling'. His draughtsman's hand lies also behind the wonderful 1/5 scale model of Cook's 'Endeavour' so splendidly exhibited in the Middlesborough town centre. Our mutual interest in 'things nautical' has guaranteed instant rapport during all discussions.

The fine results of patient and painstaking application to the photographic work by Cyril Cook and Eric Andrews of Whitby, reinforces aspects above and will certainly encourage the modeller on to the finished product. It has been sheer pleasure to meet with these two retired friends whose keen and kindly interest in my task often provided a gentle, necessary spur – those odd occasions when the spirit flagged!

Jack Jackson of Robin Hood's Bay, an extraordinarily talented violin maker and teacher of violin playing in addition, is responsible for a number of very useful 'items' that I continually reach for during S.I.B. making sessions. His sophisticated transformation of tools that I once used in earlier crude versions – notably the putty roller/tamper and the upright flattener, decimates overall working time. A close friend of long standing, my thanks to him extend beyond the confines of this book for his many kindnesses in the past.

Many occasions arose when specialist advice was completely indispensible and, in this respect, I am indebted to Tony Bearpark and fellow Directors at Maritime House in Hull. I am delighted with City Ensign's first-rate treatment of the photographic reproduction, grateful for their help in many other ways and for the exceptional interest taken in the book itself.

With the text, illustrations and photographic work completed, I was then enormously relieved to place the entire layout and final organisation into the capable hands of Graham Boddy (also of City Ensign). Graham urged me on from time to time whenever visiting Robin Hood's Bay, and directed the complicated routine for printing and publication. My book would have been produced later, rather than sooner, also less attractively without his irresistible enthusiasm and fine ideas.

An author with wife/working partner who understands fully every subtlety of text stands to great advantage and in the latter stages of pulling my book together, I have been completely content to hand over the steering wheel to my indefatigable 1st class First Mate. Without Pat's involvement, limitless determination, and her occasional 'encouraging' crack of the cat o' nine tails, my manuscript would still be lying in the drawer.

A final word of thanks to my daughter, Catherine, for the inspiration she provided initially – that day when she approached me and queried: 'Dad, will you design a ship in bottle for me – one I would be capable of making, and could be proud of afterwards?'

INTRODUCTION

ABOUT THE AUTHOR
(and his family).

by John Burden,
President, European
Association of Ships
in Bottles.
1984-1988

It is with pleasure I write the introduction to this new and innovative book which will, I am sure, prove to be of interest and value to novice and expert alike. Although I met the author only in recent years my knowledge of him and his family goes back much further, for he has figured prominently in the Ship in Bottle world for many years. It was for this reason that I approached, and was successful, in persuading him to become editor of "Bottleship", the quarterly journal of the European Association, which serves to link members in every corner of the world – makers, collectors and enthusiasts alike.

Some many years ago, Léon, throwing all caution to the winds forsook his office desk to pursue, full time, a long held interest in Arts and Crafts – originally setting up a suitable establishment in Hull, his home town, from which to operate. A well directed advert in an American nautical magazine helped to ensure the successful launch of this venture, which in turn led to a change of location. This was moved to its present idyllic setting in a seventeenth century cottage on the edge of the sea at Robin Hood's Bay, an eminently appropriate location for such a venture. The enterprise has since grown to include an exhibition centre, which the family created from a derelict chapel. This includes a heritage room, shipping wing and an auditorium complete with nine foot concert grand piano.

One could not talk about Léon, however, without direct reference to his wife and daughter, for in the many varied activities that punctuate his life, they are inextricably bound. Each member of the Labistour 'Crew' works ship whilst, individually, still finding time to do their own thing – invariably with the other's help and encouragement.

His main encouragement is, of course, from his talented wife, Patricia, very much the working partner with a multitude of talents and a life long curiosity concerning the ship in a bottle puzzle. Her own highly individualistic modelling, which reflects her interest in music, history and craftwork generally, has been exhibited at prestigious venues, given TV coverage on several occasions and is now housed permanently in the exhibition centre.

Reference to the grand piano allows me to introduce their daughter, Catherine, now pursuing a promising musical career, whose dexterous fingers and interest in the craft have inspired the second chapter of this book.

For some twenty-five years now, Léon and Pat have operated as a working partnership from their chosen cottage home, in studios standing atop an olde worlde street, commanding spectacular views across one of the most beautiful bays in England. My own impression, when visiting, is of a distinct 'On Board' atmosphere.

Léon's book arrives opportunely, for in the past decade, there has been a tremendous resurgence of interest in ship bottling throughout the world. His innovative, thoughtful and comprehensive approach to the subject is to be thoroughly recommended to anyone wishing to join us in this fascinating and totally absorbing hobby.

John Burden

Pewsey, Wiltshire.

PHOTOGRAPHS

PLANS

LINE DRAWINGS

CHAPTER 1
TOOLS & MATERIALS

AT FIRST SIGHT, the list of tools and materials for ship in bottle making might appear somewhat daunting. Don't be put off, however – many of the items listed can be found around the home eg. scissors, tweezers, pliers, etc. or can easily be substituted – metal coat hanger wire will adapt, for instance, into manipulating tools. Many other items can be dispensed with altogether. What you are looking at is really an ideal collection – one you will no doubt build up to in the course of time. (Photograph No. 1)

Be assured, it really is a cheap hobby to get started on.

TOOLS

1. **Knife** – what suits you best. I use a Stanley 'Slimline' with 5901 blades. It fits the hand perfectly.
2. **Plane** – small as possible (one that fits the hand).
3. **Chisel** – a) ¼'' for hollowing out decks. b) **Gouge** – supplements the chisel.
4. **Needles** – No. 10 with short eye ('sharps').
5. **Tweezers** – various.
6. **Metal Knitting Needles** – type that bends easily into various useful shapes.
7. **Pliers** – normal type that incorporates wire cutter.
8. **Wire cutters** – to supplement pliers.
9. **Spokeshave** – **round bottomed.**
10. **Vice** – with 1/8'' thick, card-faced jaws.
11. **Pin Vices** – appropriate for using Nos 75, 70, 1/32'' and 3/32'' drills.
12. **Scissors** – small variety.
13. **Paint brushes** – the best artists quality you can afford. (small)
14. **MISCELLANEOUS:** obvious things like rulers, pencils, pens, rubber.
15. **Trysquare** – small.
16. **'Scratch-stock'** – see page 37.
17. **Scribing tool** – illustrated.
18. **Thumb stall**
19. **Pricking tool** – eg. compasses.
20. **Metal Draw Plate** – see page 18.
21. **¼'' dowel for putty transference**
22. **Putty roller/flattener** – illustrated.
23. **Sacking Needle** – for making Turk's head knots – illustrated.

PHOTOGRAPH No. 1

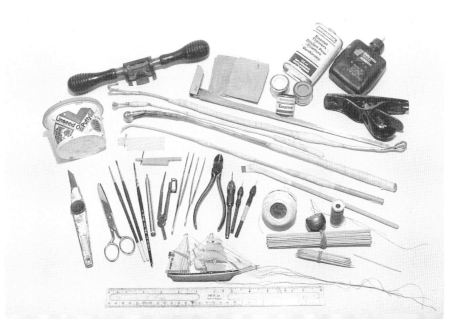

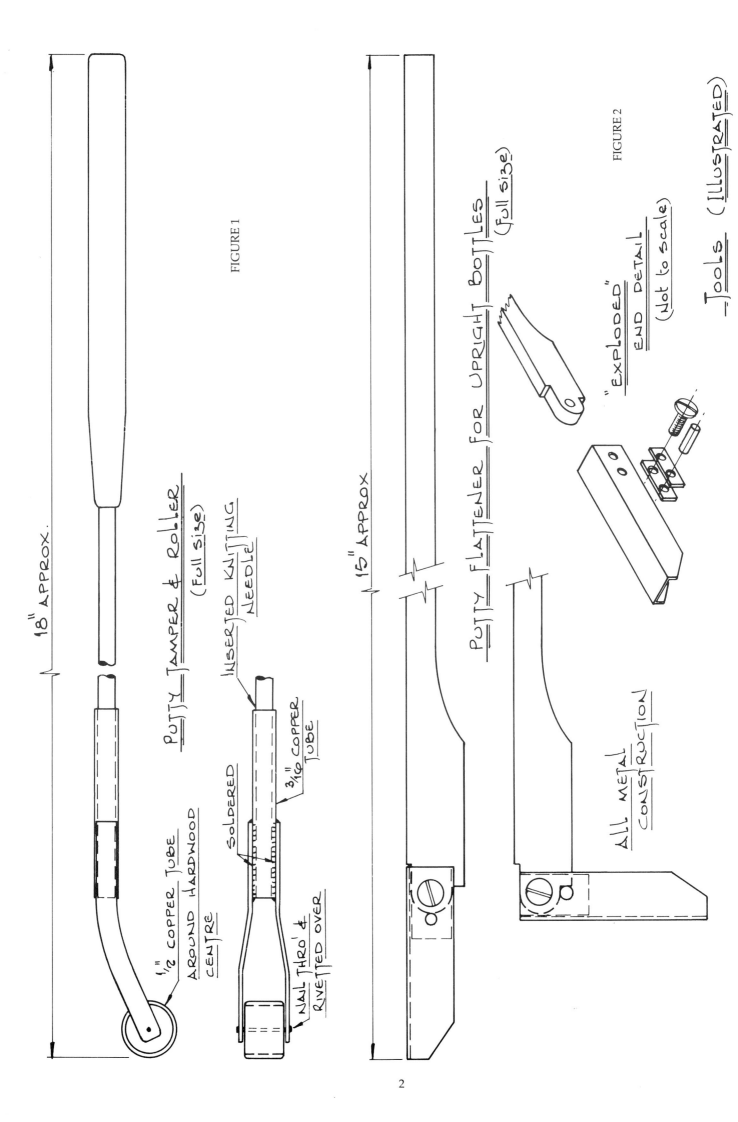

18" APPROX.

PUTTY TAMPER & ROLLER
(Full size)

FIGURE 1

INSERTED KNITTING
NEEDLE

SOLDERED

3/16" COPPER
TUBE

1/2" COPPER TUBE
AROUND HARDWOOD
CENTRE

NAIL THRO' &
RIVETTED OVER

15" APPROX.

PUTTY FLATTENER FOR UPRIGHT BOTTLES
(Full size)

FIGURE 2

"EXPLODED"
END DETAIL
(Not to scale)

Tools (ILLUSTRATED)

ALL METAL
CONSTRUCTION

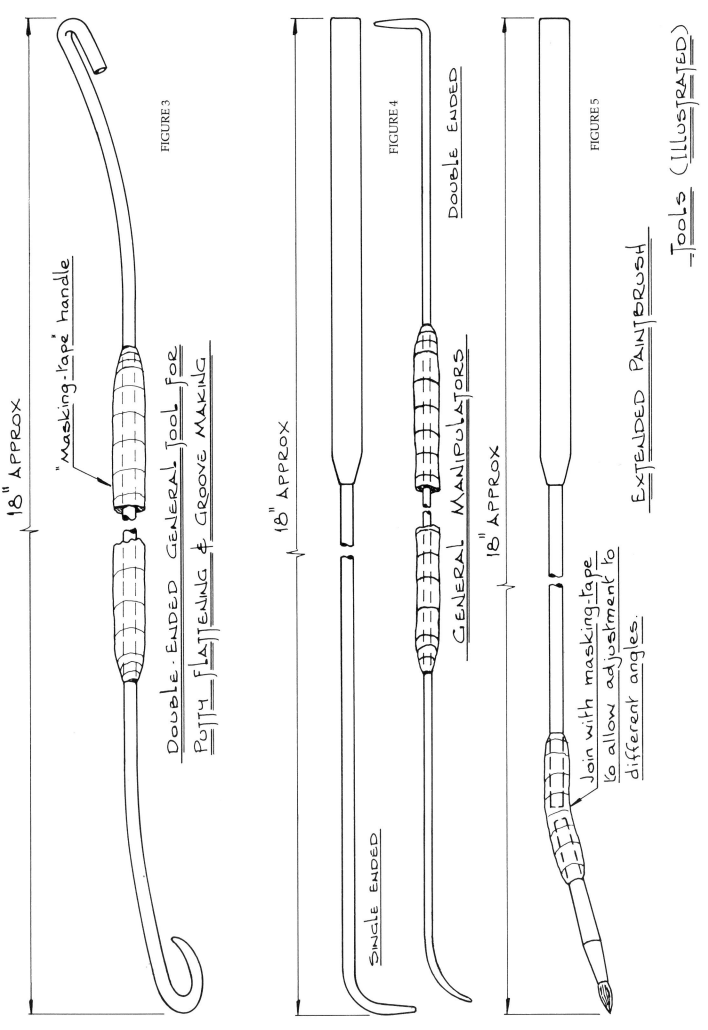

18" APPROX

"masking-tape" handle

FIGURE 3

<u>Double-Ended General Tool for</u>
<u>Putty Flattening & Groove Making</u>

18" APPROX

FIGURE 4

<u>Double Ended</u>

<u>Single Ended</u>

<u>General Manipulators</u>

18" APPROX

FIGURE 5

Join with masking-tape
to allow adjustment to
different angles.

<u>Extended Paintbrush</u>

<u>Tools (Illustrated)</u>

3

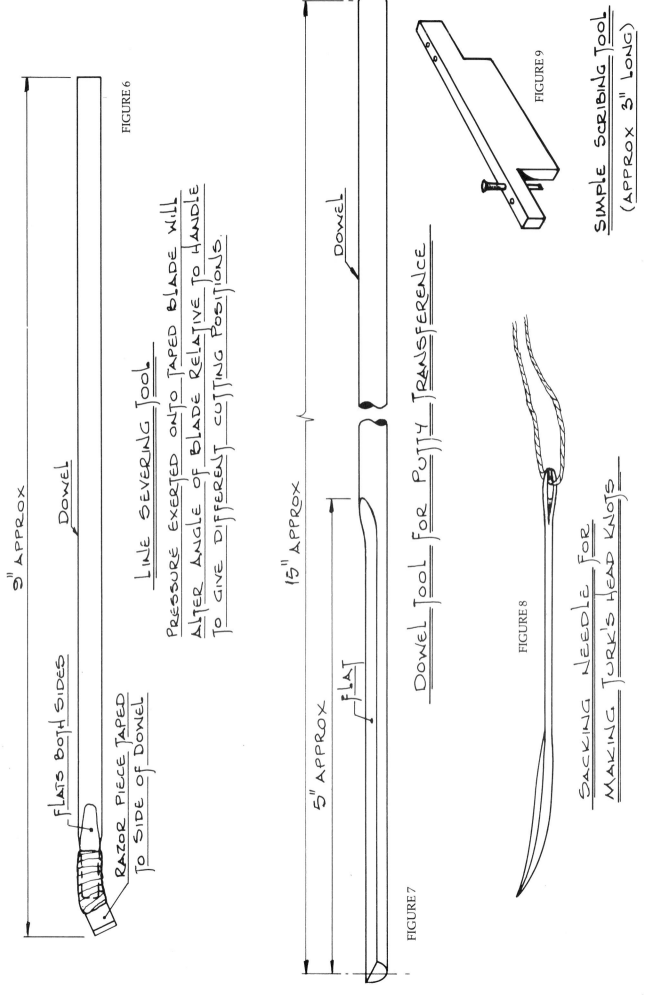

9" APPROX

Dowel

FIGURE 6

Flats Both Sides

Razor Piece Taped
To Side of Dowel

Line Severing Tool

Pressure exerted onto taped blade will
alter angle of Blade relative to handle
to give different cutting positions.

15" APPROX

Dowel

5" APPROX

Flat

FIGURE 7

Dowel Tool for Putty Transference

FIGURE 8

Sacking Needle for
Making Turk's Head Knots

FIGURE 9

Simple Scribing Tool

(Approx 3" Long)

Tools (Illustrated)

4

A BOTTLE HOLDER STAND

Although for many years I performed all 'bottling' activity quite contentedly on a flat table or cradle stand, it was not until the necessity arose, in recent years, to elevate demonstration models for better public viewing that I approached Jack Jackson (see acknowledgements) for ideas.

His creation accommodates a tapered bottle neck perfectly, leaving me in an extremely desirable 'both hands free' situation. The serious modeller would do well to copy this example which has proved a very useful addition to my equipment. (Fig. 10, Photo No. 2)

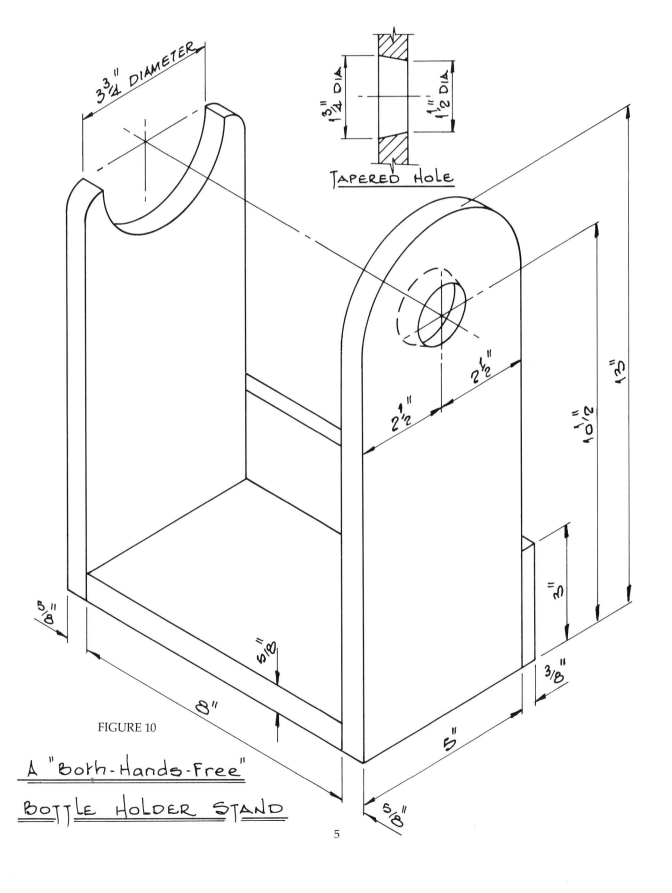

$3\frac{3}{4}$" DIAMETER

$1\frac{3}{4}$" DIA $\quad$ $1\frac{1}{2}$" DIA

TAPERED HOLE

$2\frac{1}{2}$"

$2\frac{1}{2}$"

13"

$10\frac{1}{2}$"

3"

$\frac{5}{8}$"

$\frac{5}{8}$"

$\frac{3}{8}$"

8"

5"

$\frac{5}{8}$"

FIGURE 10

A "Both-Hands-Free"

BOTTLE HOLDER STAND

5

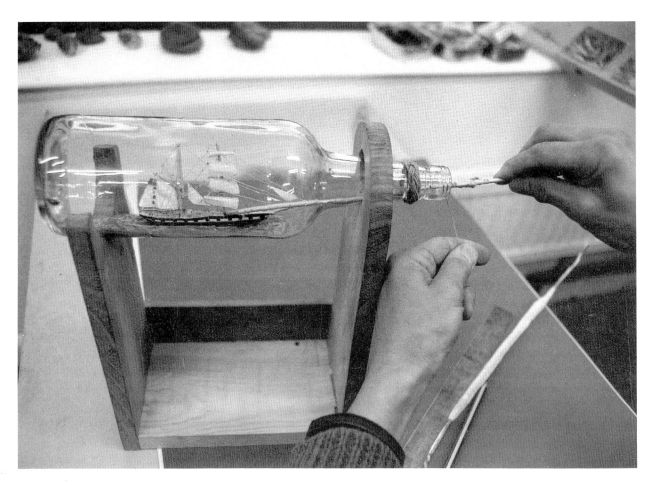

PHOTOGRAPH No. 2

MATERIALS

1. **Wood** – obeche, spruce and jelutong *can be bought in hobby shops* in various sizes.
2. **Sandpaper** – medium to light grades.
3. **Paints** – Humbrol enamels: black, white, red, green, light brown (all matt) with enamel thinners for cleaning brushes, etc.
4. **Pencils** – 6H, 9H.
5. **Paints** – **water colour** – a reasonable quality paint box or odd tubes for flags, sail paper etc.
6. **Threads** – crochet thread No. 100 (white and/or ecru) Gutermans 100% polyester sewing machine thread.
7. **Glue** – white PVA woodworkers glue.
8. **Putty** – ordinary 'household', coloured with Universal colourisers (blue, green, black).
9. **Sail paper** – 'Basildon Bond' UNLINED airmail stationery.
10. **Monofilament bristles** – from toothbrushes, hairbrushes etc, for davits, dolphin strikers, bollards, etc.
11. **Cocktail sticks** – or **1/16″** and **1/8″ dowel** – for masts, etc.
12. **Medical applicator sticks** – for yards only.
13. **Hinge wire** – guitar E string (thin).
14. **Masking tape**
15. **Bottles** 1 litre bottles only – such as Famous Grouse, Bell's, Teacher's, etc.
    Upright bottles – Pusser's Rum, Chivas Regal whisky etc.

CHAPTER 2

"BEGINNER'S MODEL"

THE AVERAGE MODELLER will, on approach to a new hobby, be "all of a rush" to get started – and this I understand perfectly, for I was (and still am to some extent) of that same nature.

Assuming then, that you have carefully read Chapter 1 and acquired the necessary tools and materials for a start, the only proviso I make before saying "let's go!" is THAT YOU FOLLOW ALL THE ENSUING METHODS, ROUTINES AND SEQUENCES. In doing so you will obviate the possible pitfalls that can normally accompany this craft, and you will be taking the easiest and best possible route to an attractive first model – one in which are incorporated many of my time-proven techniques that apply equally throughout the book.

It is, essentially, a 'teaching model' and was drawn up, initially, for the Author's daughter who successfully completed it at the tender age of 11 years 1 month (her own precise statistics). The result, (see rear cover and Photo No. 17) has done round trips to International Exhibitions, both in the U.S.A. and Japan and excites much comment from visitors to my Studio, where it is permanently seen.

Before commencement of the work, however, it is important that you should understand the **basic method used for ALL models.**
Simply stated: each ship, when completed, is placed into a bottle where the sea is already well hardened. A recess in the sea, formed by a dummy hull at the puttying stage, conveniently and neatly receives the model on to a thin spread of thickish glue which takes a firm hold in remarkably short time, provided you have followed the instructions. Following entry into the bottle, which involves collapsing the masts on wire hinges, there are, of course, great advantages in being able to manipulate the model, completely at leisure, into ship-shape form. And, by this routine, it remains clean!

From the above, it will be clear that 'household' putty (and nothing else) should be used for creating the sea. Knead it well by hand, having introduced into it just the right amounts of Universal colouriser to produce whatever shade of sea you favour. I use varying amounts of blue, green and black. Work on wads of old newspaper – if your putty is too soft, press it out on the paper which will quickly absorb some of the linseed oil content and help you on to a final optimum consistency, somewhat dough-like. Make up sufficient for several models as a ready 'store' of hardened seas is useful. In fact, acquire the habit of duplicating on all aspects of work – it's a good one and in the Beginner's case, excellent for familiarisation with materials and tools.

Make sure that your **1 litre** capacity bottles are clean, perfectly dry and free from serious distortions on the 'viewing side' before progressing now, to the real work:
Refer always to the illustrative panel (Photo No. 3) which clearly shows the sequence for making seas for all models. You will require a dummy hull ready for use. It can be made fairly quickly as there is no need to be meticulous. Make it exactly as you would a normal hull but omit thinning down of the bulwarks. Basic shape is all that is required – remember that this same hull will be used over and over again for other models, so keep it safe somewhere, wiped clean.

If you feel ambitious and opt to place a message in the bottle first, it will indicate a clear central path on which to position the sea. Make it about 3" x ½" and use black waterproof ink on typing paper. With the paintbrush, spread white PVA glue down the seam inside the bottle over an area slightly larger than your panel and then tamp it down flat, finishing off with a smearing of glue on the top. This ensures adhesion of the sea which should not be introduced into the bottle until the area is completely dried out, at which stage the writing will have reappeared, sharp and bright. The drying process can, in fact, be hastened with artificial heat. Why not make up several?

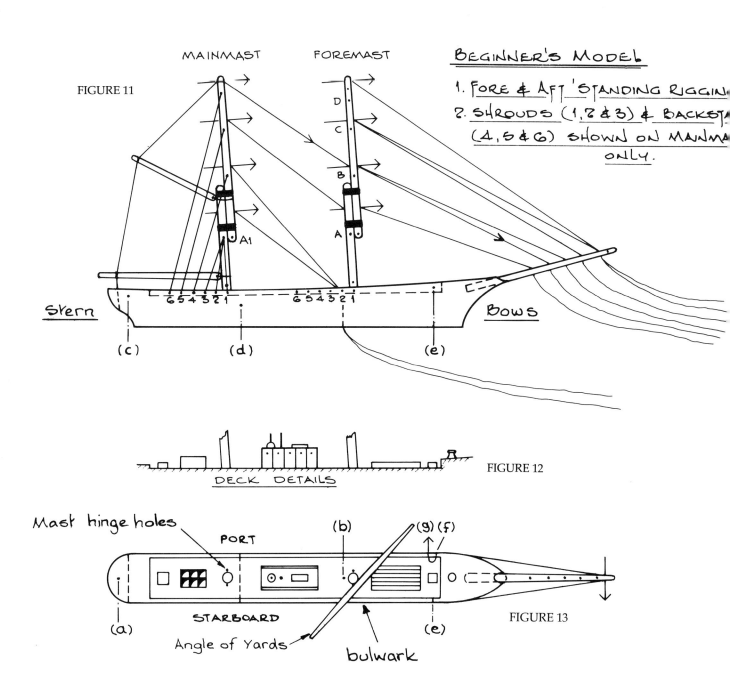

MAINMAST   FOREMAST

FIGURE 11

BEGINNER'S MODEL

1. FORE & AFT 'STANDING RIGGIN[
2. SHROUDS (1,2 & 3) & BACKST[
   (4, 5 & 6) SHOWN ON MAINMA[
   ONLY.

D

C

B

A

A1

Stern   6 5 4 3 2 1   6 5 4 3 2 1   Bows

(c)   (d)   (e)

FIGURE 12

DECK DETAILS

Mast hinge holes   PORT   (b)   (g) (f)

STARBOARD

(a)   FIGURE 13

Angle of Yards   bulwark

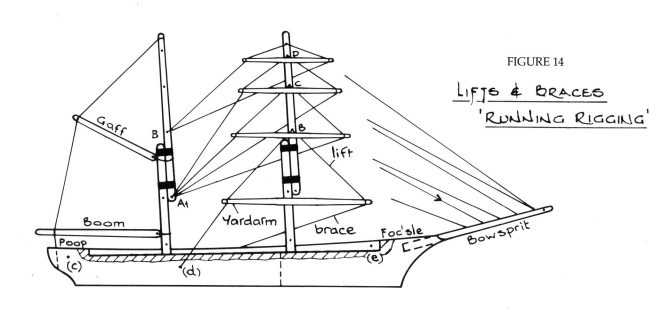

FIGURE 14

LIFTS & BRACES
'RUNNING RIGGING'

D

C

Gaff   B   B

lift

A1

Boom   Yardarm   brace   Foc'sle   Bowsprit

Poop

(c)   (d)   (e)

8

Correct depth of sea is important and a 'sausage' of coloured putty 6″ x 5/16″ diameter, when flattened out evenly to 6″ x 1″, achieves just this. Use your dowel tool to place the sausage centrally down the seam of the bottle – cut it into 3 pieces if you find this easier. Transference is quite simple if you gently press, first on the putty to attach to the dowel and then again on the bottle interior, to detach. Select whatever tools suit you best for flattening out the sea, forming waves and 'bedding down' the hull. (Refer to panel-photo No. 3)

Sequence
1. Sea flattened and waves being formed. (A thin coating of white paint, streaked with black, blends with the sea to produce a more interesting finish).
2. Waves completed and rocks 'bedded' on an extended area. Note hole for lighthouse.
3. 'Bedding' the dummy hull is somewhat easier if a narrow locating groove is first made centrally on the waves. Press it down gently with a very slight to-and-fro rocking motion by inserting tip of tool into indentations. This illustration shows a tool in position for 'springing out' the hull. This is done with a quick upward flick of the wrist, after which a minimum of tidying should be all that is necessary.
4. The final result, as it would appear in the bottle with a simple lighthouse glued in.

PHOTOGRAPH No. 3

MAKING THE HULL

Creation of a well-shaped hull with attractive 'sheer' (Fig. 23) and fine bulwarks (Fig. 24) is absolutely essential to the appearance of finished models. This can be achieved, easily and quickly, if you follow the sequence depicted in Figs. 15 to 24. Don't despair if you haven't a vice:- for hollowing the deck, simply sandwich your block of wood between 2 lengths of the same, nailed to your bench with an end stop. For planing, screw the jig to a board 6" x 3" x ½" and clamp it on the bench end. Any reasonable size of plane can utilised but one that fits the hand must be regarded as optimum for the miniature modeller. Removal of the 'meat' to the basic shape, followed by sanding, is rapid and extremely satisfying. If you don't possess a plane, I can only suggest that short of using a chisel or whittling-knife, you borrow one – taking the opportunity to make up several hulls at the same time. But, do return it quickly, cleaned and sharpened, as you will certainly need it again. (I really ought to say at this point, that you are going to get 'hooked' on S.I.B. making!)

CHOOSING THE WOOD

Since discovering JELUTONG, choice of wood for me is no longer a matter for consideration. It is light in weight (yet strong), carves beautifully, sands, paints and drills easily. Its impeccable behaviour is particularly appreciated when reducing thickness of bulwarks, having none of the 'wayward' characteristics of many other types of wood. (The correct way to fine down bulwarks is described later).

There are, of course, many usable woods readily available in good hobby shops (eg. Obeche) and ½" x ½", the size we work from, is 'standard'.

USING THE PLAN

A few words about the PLAN drawings (Figs. 11 to 14). Briefly, your completed hull should equate near enough to these shapes and outlines. Don't worry, however, about slight discrepancies here and there – all repetitive hand-made articles vary to some extent, one from the next, and our aim is principally to produce a hull that 'looks right', of dimensions that accommodate to the bottle. Use the plan to test your side view and a template of the underside, flat area, to confirm your knife-work.

PHOTOGRAPH No. 4

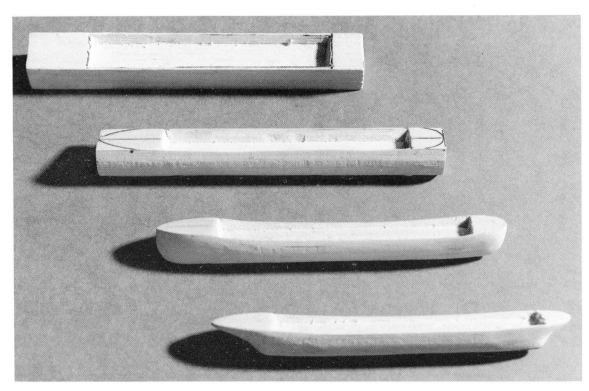

SEQUENCE FOR MAKING HULL (Figs. A to G)

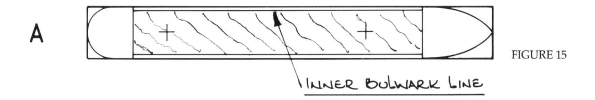

A

FIGURE 15

INNER BULWARK LINE

A. Smooth all sides of a ½″ x ½″ block of wood – 4½″ long. Mark one side as at Fig. A and remove the shaded area to a depth of 5/32″ (Make a card template to measure depth accurately). This involves straightforward chisel work – (a ¼″ wide would be ideal) after first making cross-cuts at both ends and scoring down the inner bulwark line with a knife. Afterwards fold small squares of sandpaper into handy shapes to produce a nice, smooth finish to the deck and ends. Great advantages are gained with a SCRIBER TOOL (see 'Tools and Materials'). I recommend that you make one, sometime. A little practice makes perfect. It is easy to make and worth its weight in gold. Mine was given to me by my violin-making friend, as were several more items that he designed and made, some from my own rough drawings and ideas.

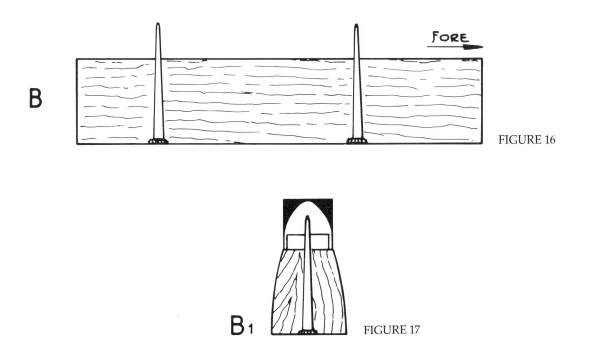

B

FORE

FIGURE 16

B₁

FIGURE 17

B. Prick holes where indicated on deck with a compass point and mount up on the jig (Fig. B) in the vice. NB. The protruding panel pins stand 3/8″ clear of the jig – just sufficient for a firm hold. Mark the ends as at B1, draw in a centre line and then, with an extra fine setting on your plane, take off the black areas, afterwards sanding to a very smooth, clean finish.

Remove carefully from the jig.

C   FIGURE 18

C. The black areas between the bulwark ends should now be clearly, and accurately marked in. Carefully remove these with a sharp knife, taking off too little rather than too much. Tidy up with sandpaper – then leave alone, for later.

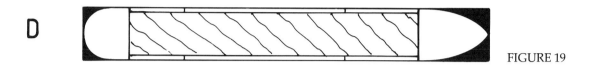

D   FIGURE 19

D. Carve the ends round black areas.

E   FIGURE 20

E. Mark in the black portions and remove with a knife.

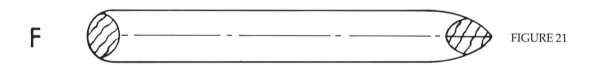

F   FIGURE 21

F. Draw in centre line under the bows. Apply the knife as at Photo No. 5 to carve down to the required shapes. Study all photographs. Smooth with sandpaper. Note author's use of thumb-stall (Photo No. 5).

G   FIGURE 22

G. Mark in the black areas, then carefully knife off the top side so that the depth of bulwark at both ends is reduced and a nice flowing sheerline is produced. (Don't worry about a small discrepancy in bulwark depth for'ard).

Then, knife off the black portion under the hull, leaving a flat surface. This should approximate to the plan template. If necessary, put in a centre line, draw on the template shape and carve down to it. Sand and smooth all surfaces.

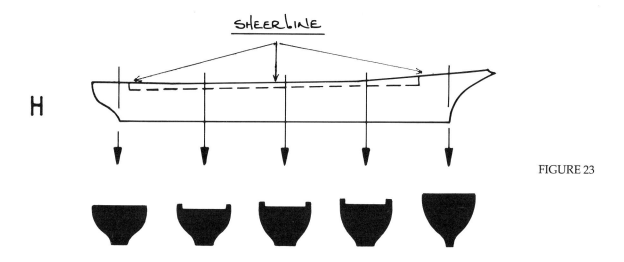

SHEERLINE

FIGURE 23

H

TEMPLATE FOR UNDERSIDE

The silhouettes at 'H' represent cross-sections through the hull at those points indicated by the linking lines.

PHOTOGRAPH No. 5

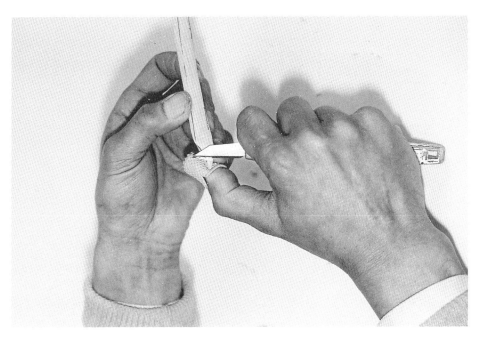

THE BOWSPRIT

Mark and carve out the small curved recess to take a 'stump' (one part) tapered bowsprit made from a cocktail stick. Use a 3/32″ drill to make a hole ½″ deep in which to insert and glue the bowsprit, angled upwards to follow the sheerline.

CREATING FINE BULWARKS

It is good policy for all models to leave this, the most delicate job, until last. Fine looking bulwarks enhance a model and **can** be achieved, whilst still retaining their strength in spite of a multiplicity of holes drilled through them. Mine invariably finish off at less than ½mm at the 'capping'.

One simply carves away surplus material AT AN ANGLE so that thickness and strength are retained at deck level where drilling takes place. Photo No. 6 depicts what I consider the best technique, direction of cut being changed when 'humouring the grain' is called for.

Naturally, the Beginner and others should only attempt what they feel capable of, but ultimately, you can knife down to a razor-edge – then restore the capping by gentle sanding. (Fig. 24)

PHOTOGRAPH No. 6

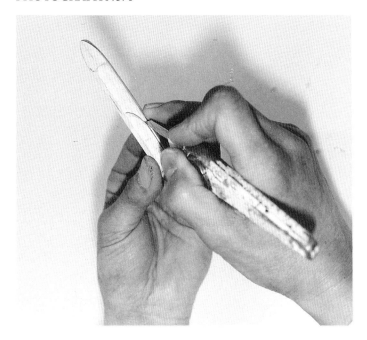

FIGURE 24

ENLARGED SECTION
SHOWING TAPERED
BULWARKS

PREPARING THE HULL FOR MARKING AND DRILLING

Before marking for drilling, the entire hull is given a coat of matt white enamel paint. Use a brush to apply the paint – first, **very** lightly across the entire top (deck side) and then fairly liberally on the sides, bottom and ends using a finger to rub the paint in, neatly overall. Don't omit to use finger ends for laying on a broad base colour – the finish imparted is quite superior to any brush. Leave to dry thoroughly, (minimum 2 hours) then give it the lightest possible sanding.

With your fine-grade sandpaper, very gently rub down the entire top side keeping a watchful eye on the effect being produced. Leave it looking quite uneven , but subdued. Later, with the addition of lightly pencilled plank lines, a 'scrubbed deck' appearance will be simulated, the desirability of which will become more apparent when 'antiqued' sails are bent to the yards.

MARKING

All points for drilling will now be marked, then gently pricked with a compass point to guide the drills in. (Refer to plans at beginning of Chapter).

Begin by pencilling a line along the outside bulwark on which to mark the 4 sets of 6 shroud holes. Use your middle finger held against the pencil (the time-honoured carpenter's trick) to run along the capping. N.B. Check with a trysquare that port and starboard shrouds are marked exactly opposite and bear in mind that these pricked holes, when drilled, will emerge at deck level.

Now mark and prick the remaining points: e, f, and g, are positioned on the bulwarks just as the shrouds; mast hinge-holes are set 1/8" apart exactly per plan. (Fig. 13) Note – Holes a, b, and hinge holes are drilled vertically through the hull; c, and d, are drilled laterally through the solid hull. Endeavour to go through reasonably straight with these.

DRILLING

All holes should now be drilled: use a No. 70 drill for holes a, b, c and d. All others No. 75. Tidy up with light sanding where necessary.

A PIN-VICE is an almost indispensable tool for a ship modeller but, even more import-ant, is the acquisition of commercial 'needle-size' drills as you can, at a pinch, fashion your own pin-vice substitute. If you lack experience with these fine drills, do practice their use carefully – they are not exactly cheap!

Hole (b) behind the Foremast may be slightly enlarged should the modeller so wish.

PHOTOGRAPH No. 7

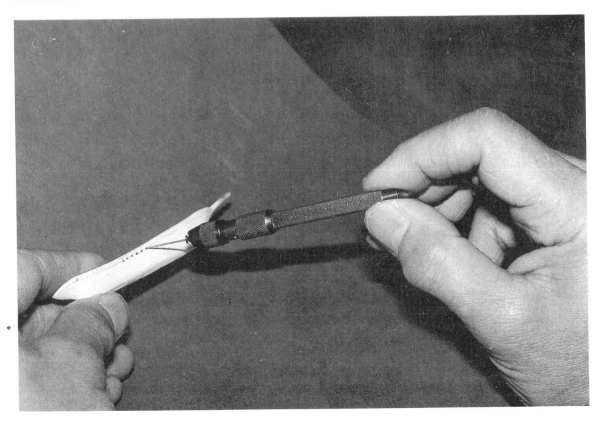

Correct way to use a Pin Vice.

"FAST ANTIQUING"

From foregoing remarks, the modeller will note my preference for a finished model with 'working atmosphere' about it, not to mention the antique look. It is, after all, an old Craft and the only genuine 'sailor made' models around today have every appearance of antiquity. This of course we can only endeavour to simulate, but a start given to it, by whatever means, certainly contributes to the ageing process that time performs naturally.

On this theme and for what it is worth, I will relate what has happened to a model I made for my wife during our courtship:

When we 'set up shop' together, it was proudly given forefront prominence in a display window – heedless of consequences we had been made aware of. The first bright sunny day produced an effect inside the bottle that filled us with dismay. The ship was hardly visible, obscured by a mass of water globules on the glass. Quickly retrieved and placed elsewhere, we were amazed to discover that within an hour everything was back to normal – completely dried out! It was like a magician's trick and engaged us in much thought.

Curiosity finally overcoming concern, the model was returned to its original position in the window where, throughout an entire heat-wave type summer, it repeated the 'miracle' daily! Fortuitously, what remains after 25 years, is a ship in bottle greatly enhanced in many respects through a naturally-hastened antiquing process. And, because an old-style bottle was utilised in the first instance, it is virtually impossible to date the model's origin accurately, within the last 100 years.

Those versed in physics can no doubt explain the mystery.

LINING DECKS

Atmosphere can now be added to **your** ship by lining the decks carefully with a finely pointed, hard pencil – 6H to 9H ideal. Put in a centre line and work the starboard side first, employing the 'carpenter's trick' again. For the Beginner, a total of 12 lines will suffice (see Photo No. 8 for method used on the curved ends). Always err on the side of subdued effect.

PHOTOGRAPH No. 8

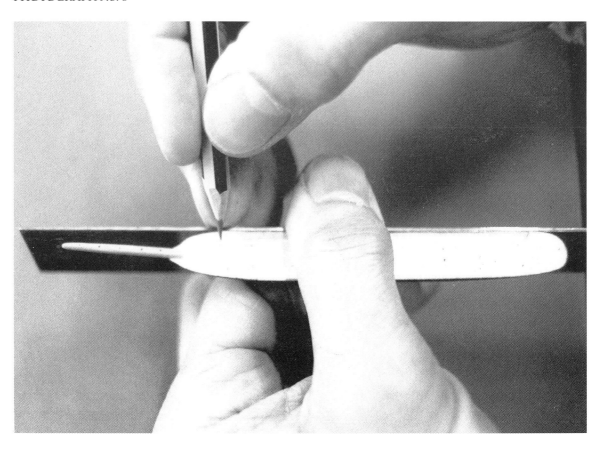

PAINTING

There is no problem to creating a neat white band around the hull. A strip of masking-tape carefully positioned and then gently but firmly thumbed down will, after painting each side of the tape, remove to reveal the desired result (Photo No. 9). Cut the lengths (about 3/32" wide) on a piece of glass, using a metal ruler and sharp blade. My own suggestion for colour scheme is black above the tape, antique red below (both matt).

Mounted on your compasses for convenience during painting, the hull can be put away to dry afterwards for 3 hours, still attached. Leave the tape in position.

One important point, finally – matt paints usually dry to a powdery-looking finish and I never omit to gently rub over all surfaces with my thumb which, in its turn, produces a more desirable, slightly burnished effect. Again, this contributes to the entire atmosphere of your model.

PHOTOGRAPH No. 9

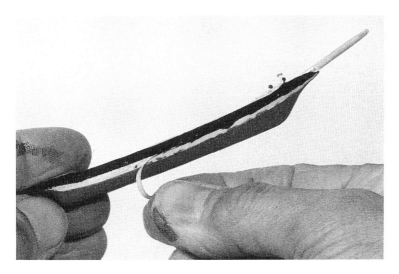

MAKING THE MASTS

Making the masts and yards is an obvious occasion for 'duplicating' on work (advocated earlier), spares being put away safely for future use, or in case of breakages.

Down to the finished mast, with yards attached and hinge inserted ready for stepping in the hull – sequence is of some importance. Follow it through. Equally, is the examination of mast material for adequate strength.

Cocktail sticks, formerly ideal for the job, have suffered severe loss in quality in recent years and you may have to resort to knife work on commercial 1/16" or 1/8" dowel.

Sequence

Both masts are identical so for each ship, make 2 upper and 2 lower parts. Mark, prick and drill (No. 70) only for the arrowed holes (Fig. 11), one in the bottom section, four in the other. Join the 2 parts, exactly per plan, by inserting a nylon bristle such as found on a toothbrush, through the 'doubling' holes. Place glue between the overlapping parts, nip up with tweezers and leave to set. If you work on a piece of glass, it will help maintain the 2 parts in a straight line.

Make sure the masts are firmly glued before further handling. Remove bristle when satisfied.

Remaining holes to drill are represented by dots on the plan and these run the opposite direction to the arrowed holes i.e. across the ship. Face your mast as on plan – mark, prick and drill. Use a No. 75 for the hinge-hole and the topmost hole – No. 70 for the other 5.

A fine band of masking tape wrapped around the 'doublings' where shown, adds unobtrusive detail and extra security.

Don't varnish masts as capillary attraction may draw varnish into the drilled holes.

17

MAKING YARDS

Strength, combined with delicacy of appearance, was an important point touched upon in the creation of bulwarks. Similarly, these same considerations apply in the production of yards which need to withstand pressures put upon the during 'bottling' and also visibly contrast in size with the masts they attach to.

Unquestionably, laborious paring with a knife of the smallest commercial dowel available is a task to obviate and the problem is simply met with a metal draw-plate. This comprises a series of varying-sized holes through which the dowel is pulled. You start with the largest hole through which the dowel can be passed and then gradually reduce it by pulling through smaller and smaller holes. My home-made version was fashioned in 10 minutes from a large washer, is fully efficient and a pleasure to use (see Fig. 25). It will reduce down to 1/32", with ease.

PHOTOGRAPH No. 10

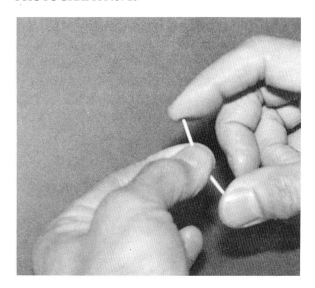

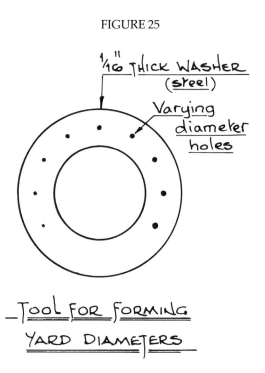

FIGURE 25

1/16" THICK WASHER (steel)

Varying diameter holes

TOOL FOR FORMING YARD DIAMETERS

For yards however, I advise use of the fibrous-natured medical applicator sticks – usually sold in boxes of 500. These smooth to a good finish and are remarkably strong. Routines soon evolve: mine is to cut up the stick into handy 3" lengths, taper the entered end with a knife and gently, but firmly, hammer it through the draw-plate about ½". Pliers, with card-faced jaws, then pull the remainder through.

Strength of yards **and** masts can always be tested as follows: support the ends between finger and thumb of right hand – grip centre with same fingers of left hand – bend back and forth. (Photo No. 10)

Make your 4 yards to lengths given on the plan, tapering the ends slightly. By whatever means the yards are thinned, final choice of thickness is left to the individual. NB. Applicator sticks are not suitable for masts.

GAFF AND BOOM

Make gaff and boom to plan size, tapering one end only. Prick and drill No. 75 holes, where indicated – 1/16" from the ends next to the mast. (Fig. 27)

INSERTING HINGES, ATTACHING YARDS AND STEPPING MASTS

Hinges are best inserted into the masts, now. For years, I used a fine guitar E string until purchasing an enormously long coil of similar guage wire in Spain some years ago – a matter of coppers and enough to last a lifetime! I cannot imagine a better wire for the job (rigid but pliable). Alas, it remains at this moment unidentified.

Meanwhile, I recommend the metal E string, so perhaps you know a friendly guitarist willing to part with 3″ off the surplus that always seems to waver around the tuning pegs! A violin E string can also be quite useable. **(a)** Cut a piece of wire approximately 1½″ – push it through the hinge-hole and middle it. **(b)** Carefully bend the wire each side of the mast to sharp right-angles so that the whole hinge hugs the side of the mast. **(c)** Clean out the deck holes with a No. 75 drill and test both masts. Trim off any wire that protrudes below the hull. (Fig. 26)

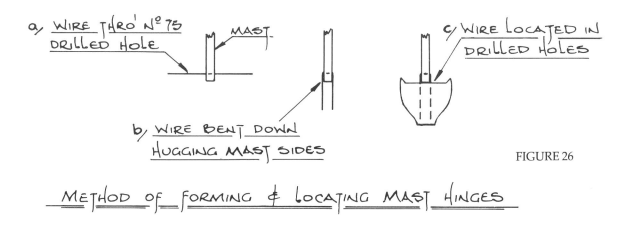

FIGURE 26

METHOD of FORMING & LOCATING MAST HINGES

Attach all four yards to the foremast where indicated on the plan: tie and double knot a six inch cotton round the centre of each yard, then tie and knot the cotton ends around the mast (Fig. 28). Angle all yards, as indicated, before glueing knots and trimming off with scissors. A spot of glue on the cottons round the mast helps to maintain the yard at the correct angle.

Thread six inch cottons through the holes in the gaff and boom and tie these with a **treble knot**. This allows the gaff and boom free movement in all directions when collapsing the masts. Afterwards, attach to the mainmast as indicated (Fig. 27)

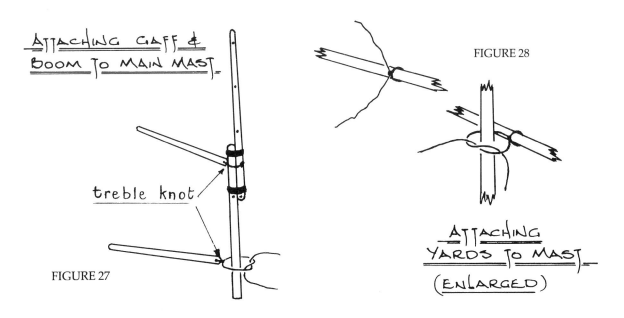

ATTACHING GAFF & BOOM TO MAIN MAST

treble knot

FIGURE 27

FIGURE 28

ATTACHING YARDS TO MAST (ENLARGED)

We now face a period of activity that involves a fair amount of needle-threading and, to quote one lady observer – 'sewing together'. Catherine's model was rigged entirely with white crochet cotton (No. 100) dyed a hempen colour, a thread I use constantly for the lower range of production models as it fulfils many requirements. Don't hesitate to look around obvious sources of supply for other suitable threads. Proprietors of needlework shops are invariably helpful, especially if you explain the precise requirements. Do, however, select subdued tones of colour and nothing heavier than the above. Don't let threading of No. 10 needles bug you – it is made quite easy (even for the mere male) by pressing some glue on the cotton end to stiffen it.

The 'stepping' process will be made considerably easier by first cleaning out all drilled holes. Tackle them carefully by inserting the No. 10 needle you will shortly be using, rubbing and twisting in each hole to produce a smooth, burnished effect – 2 minutes work for a far greater saving in time. N.B. Bring tweezers into use.

It is my considered opinion that the model is best worked entirely in the hand – and not attached to a work stand.

STEPPING OF MASTS

Now put the foremast into position using a smear of glue on the hinge if it appears too free in the holes. Thread a 20″ cotton, knot the end and take it through the top arrow-hole, thence into the first hole of the bowsprit at the tip. The mast now has to be secured at a slightly raked-back angle and, to achieve this, a few turns of the thread are made around the bowsprit end and held fast with 'back-loops' (Fig. 29). These loops are put to continued use on all models – study, and master them! For the correct way to hold your model whilst performing the whole operation, see Photo No. 11.

PHOTOGRAPH No. 11

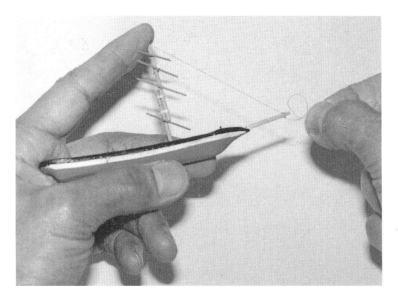

FIGURE 29

DRAWING of 'BACK LOOP'

The shrouds and backstays are now to be rigged. These are the lines that support the mast either side. N.B. Remember to keep them on the **outside** of the hull. Refer at all times to the plan. (Fig. 11)

Now, thread a 20″ length of cotton with a knot on one end. Proceed as follows keeping behind the loose yards.

1. From the inside of the bulwark, push the needle through hole No. 1 on the starboard side and draw the cotton to the outside of the ship.
2. Thread the needle through hole A in the mast and draw the cotton right through.
3. Push the needle into hole No. 1 (port side) and pull the cotton inboard.
4. Push the needle into hole No. 2 (port) from inboard and draw it through. (You are on the outside of the ship).
5. Take the needle through hole A again and draw the cotton through.
6. Push the needle into hole No. 2 (starboard) and pull the cotton inboard.
7. Push the needle, now, into hole No. 3 (starboard) from inboard and draw it through.
8. Take the needle through hole A again and draw the cotton through.
9. Push the needle into hole No. 3 and pull the cotton inboard.
10. Push the needle back outboard through hole No. 4 (port).

Keep all lines behind the yards.

11. Take the needle through hole B and draw the cotton through.
12. Push the needle into hole No. 4 (starboard) and pull the cotton inboard.
13. Push the needle back outboard through hole No. 5 (starboard).
14. Take the needle through hole C and draw the cotton through.
15. Push the needle into hole No. 5 (port) and pull the cotton inboard.
16. Push the needle back outboard through hole No. 6 (port).
17. Take the needle through hole D and draw the cotton through.
18. Push the needle into hole No. 6 and pull the cotton inboard.
19. To finish off – push the needle back outboard through the previous hole (i.e. No. 5 starboard), draw the cotton through and glue the disappearing end. Trim off when set.

PHOTOGRAPH
No. 12

Now put the mainmast into position – thread a 20″ cotton knotted at one end and take it through the top arrow-hole, thence through arrow-hole above B of the foremast and down through the bowsprit.

Holding the mast parallel with the Foremast, draw the line taut and make a few turns around the bowsprit end – securing with back-loops as before.

Take a knotted cotton from under the stern up through hole (a). Keeping the boom horizontal, secure the line with back-loops and then the gaff, finishing off at the top of the mainmast, again with back-loops, and glue.

Now rig shrouds and backstays exactly as the foremast, which is somewhat easier with no hampering yards. Referring carefully to the plan, rig out all the remaining fore-and-aft lines allowing for approximately 6″ to extend out of the bottle neck. N.B. Make sure knots are of adequate size. **This concludes the 'Standing Rigging'.**

LIFTS AND BRACES:

The lifts and braces now to be rigged on your model comprise some of the gear that would be used on a ship for supporting the yards and setting them at the required angle relative to wind direction.

Before commencing, we shall make the masts less susceptible to lateral movement by glueing at point A, both sides, (Fig. 11). Eye up for straightness, then use a finely pointed cocktail stick to apply the glue.

Sequence: Keep the plan in view as you work. (Fig. 14)

First, ensure that rigging is taut and holding the masts perfectly upright. Develop the knack of sliding lines off the bowsprit end and then re-securing them all together, with one joint 'back-loop'.

Then, lean your model against a handy-sized box, **facing right**.

1. Thread a 12" cotton. Tie and glue it around the end of the bottom yard-arm. Trim off the loose end.
2. Take the needle through B and draw the cotton through – (try not to penetrate the line already rigged in this hole).
3. Secure at the other yard-arm end with back-loops (glue for safety) then take the needle through hole (d) to emerge on the starboard side of the ship.
4. Angle the yard as per plan (Fig. 13) – take a couple of turns around the yard end where you started from and secure with back loops. Glue and trim off.

This is the pattern to rig out the 3 remaining yards. Follow the plan and try to keep all lines reasonably taut. Note, that 2 braces go through A1. Release bowsprit lines and test that the masts will collapse.

This concludes the 'Running Rigging'.

SAILS

Sails with a 'used' appearance are now added to the ship and this is achieved by 'antiquing' normal-weight, white airmail paper – unruled, of course – eg. Basildon Bond or W. H. Smith's.

My own routine is to make up a complete pad, applying to both sides of the paper, a wash made up from yellow ochre water colour broken with a spot of black. Try using a cotton-wool ball for quick and easy application of the wash. Basically, we are aiming to just remove the stark whiteness of the paper. Alternatively, black coffee is a handy substitute. But, remember to always err on the side of subdued effect.

When the paper is perfectly dry and flat, cover the entire sheet with lines drawn 1/16" apart using a 6H to 9H pencil. Ideally, they should be only just discernible.

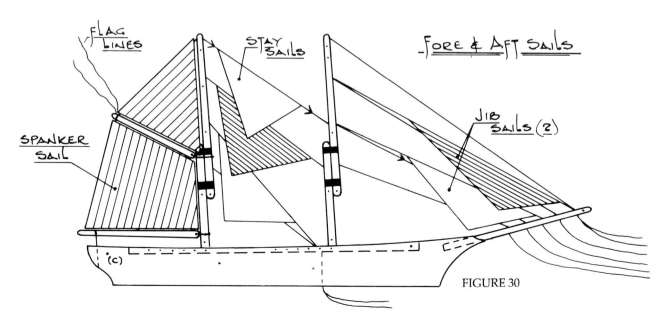

FIGURE 30

Cut your spanker sail first and the one above it. 'Tailor' them to fit exactly, then spread a thin line of glue on the cotton to press the sail on. (Fig. 30)

Cut out the three stay-sails between the masts according to plan sizes and then press each one individually around a pencil to produce a curved effect. Proceed, by glueing the bottom sail first on the cotton: hold it with your tweezers, run a line of glue along the edge to be attached – carefully place on the stay-line and press it down with the 'wrong' end of the tweezers. The other two sails should just neatly overlap. Manoeuvre the yards out of the way and if the curve in any sail proves a nuisance, press it gently out as it can be encouraged back to shape later on, quite easily.

This same routine applies with the jib-sails. The four remaining square sails (Fig. 31) should be cut slightly deeper than plan size, (to allow for curvature), pressed around a pencil and then glued to the front edge of the yards. 'Tailor' them to look right, leaving small ends of yards showing – approx. 1mm.

FIGURE 31

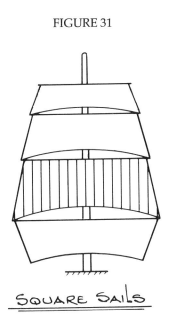

SQUARE SAILS

FLAG LINE

Take a 10" cotton, tie and glue where indicated (Fig. 30) letting the ends hang down. Thread each end in turn and take them through hole (c) from opposite sides. Pull them taut, then withdraw each one about ½". Now smear glue on, pull back taut again and leave to set before trimming off.

Attach flags of your own choosing both on the flag-line and at mast trucks. Be authentic, if possible, eg. the signal I use to accompany the 'Red Duster' flies the message 'We wish you a pleasant voyage' from Capt. Marryatt's Merchant Code of the period. Use fairly bold, but dull colours – particularly red, as it rates a high 'fugitive'. (For your interest, I have twice replaced the Ensign of my wife's model – a rather tricky operation!). (see page 29).

DECK FITTINGS

The main item will be a deckhouse midships, painted pale brown – one end suggesting the galley and the other, accommodation. Mark with a pencil as shown, and simulate portholes by pressing a sharp compass point tipped with white paint into the wood.

Study the deck plan for other suggestions. (Figs. 12 & 13) N.B. All fittings can be glued in position except the deckhouse which is included after bottling.

SETTING THE YARDS

Before 'bottling', yards are all set to the correct angle and held, by placing a spot of glue port and starboard where the braces penetrate (d) through the hull and A1 and B on the main mast. (Fig. 14)

At this stage, examine your model carefully to see that all is 'shipshape' and nothing omitted, etc. Make sure that the 2 lines penetrating the deck at (b) move freely in and out. Swivel each yard on its lift to confirm free movement also and ALL sails should then be coaxed back to a gentle curve by using tweezers. (Leave the Spanker).

BOTTLING

The moment of truth, and for the faint-hearted, let me bolster your confidence:– in the course of raising funds for a favourite charity, I have demonstrated a model of this same design being put into the same bottle approx. 4,000 times during one summer season.

Speed, in the middle of a working day, is essential, and the gimmicky routine of 1: removing the erected model from the bottle, 2: erecting it outside the bottle with one hand, 3: collapsing and returning to its original state inside the bottle – is performed in a total of thirteen seconds!

Fortunately, you can take your time!

So, now put your bottle in front of you, facing right – likewise your model.

Study the illustrations. (Photo's 13, 14, 15)

Release all lines and gently push back the masts, at the same time swivelling the 4 yards so that each sail overlaps the one below it. As the masts are coming down, curve the Spanker sail slightly pushing it towards you. That way, it receives minimum crushing.

On a simple model such as this, there is no real necessity to force the 'top hamper' down absolutely flat (i.e. the masts, yards, etc.). Insert your ship into the bottle, taking care to guide in the tip of the boom and you will discover that pressure from the bottle itself, will flatten the top hamper just the required amount.

Depending on the shape of the bottle neck, it should be possible to bring up the masts slightly on the way in by gently 'teasing' on the cottons.

PHOTOGRAPH No. 13

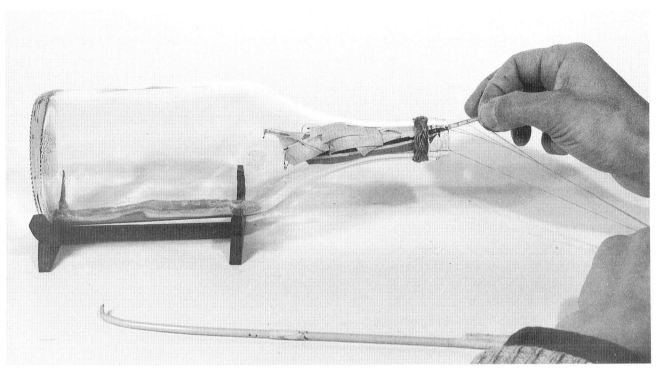

PHOTOGRAPH No. 14

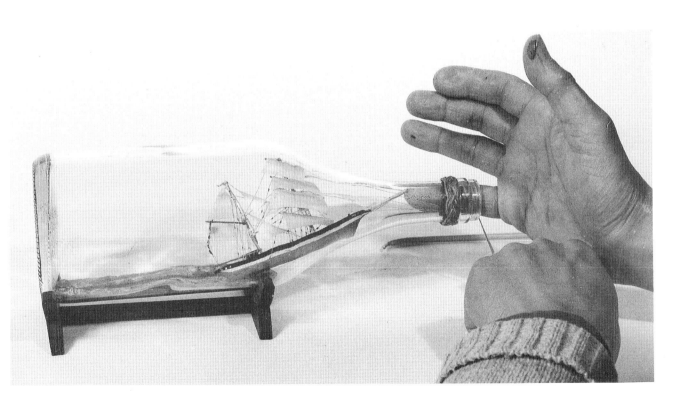

PHOTOGRAPH No. 15

Study the photograph for perfect method – noting tip of bowsprit held under the nail of little finger.

You can now tilt the bottle, letting your ship down behind the sea which should be dried out fairly hard.

Choose a double-ended wire (one end slightly rounded, the other at a right-angle) and take your time in bringing the ship back upright. Use the square end to gently gain leverage on the cottons where they emerge under the hull and bowsprit. Pressures that you exert should always be tentative.

To some extent, you are on to your own initiative now. In all probability everything will be 'plain sailing' but if, for example, the masts resist erection, look for a line that may be tipped over the mainmast or, a 'fouled' flag-line. You can, of course, always push the masts down again to assist release.

With all the lines drawn through their respective holes and the yards squared off – we now apply a very useful technique for 'losing' the two cottons under the hull: withdraw these two to three inches out of the deck hole and apply a light smear of glue to be taken back down the hole immediately after, again using the right-angled tool in the manner previously described. Manipulate the bottom yard to clear the way.

After ½ hour, a mounted razor piece will cut off the cottons flush under the hull, leaving the mainmast effectively held upright. This technique is particularly appreciated on a 4 masted barque where 3 pairs of cottons are removed 'at a stroke'. (Fig. 32)

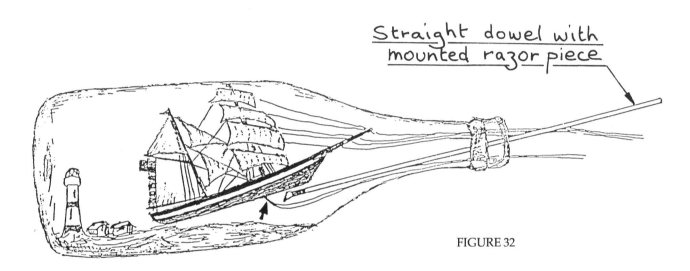

Straight dowel with mounted razor piece

FIGURE 32

'BEDDING' THE SHIP

Exposure of white woodworker's glue on a jar top will, with occasional stirring, eventually thicken to a consistency suitable for 'bedding' the ship on. Ideally, it should be quite stiff, yet transferable in small amounts to the putty recess with a wire tool. Spread it evenly, keeping the ship out of the way, and don't overdo the amount. Then, edge your model to the recess, manipulate it over and in, gently pressing down on the deck to leave it perfectly upright. Keep it straight for 24 hours and don't worry about small quantities of glue that may ooze out around the hull – these will press down, or remove, after the initial setting. It will, anyway, dry out colourless. Note: glue accidently left on glass removes fairly easily with a wire tool, when dry.

REMOVING BOWSPRIT LINES

With the ship firmly established (and not until) draw the bowsprit lines taut and tidy the yards. Now push the tautened lines back out of their holes about 3/16", apply a smear of white glue around the cottons and draw back again. Hold them fast by securing with a piece of masking tape just outside the bottle. Clean off any surplus glue on the bowsprit and then leave for 3 to 4 hours before attempting to remove them.

(At times such as this, the best remedy for impatience is to get on with work towards your next model!)

Design of a 'severing' tool is largely dependent on the bottle's shape – more often than not, you will get away with a piece of razor-blade taped to a straight dowel. otherwise, tape it to a wire that will bend to the shape required. Make sure that lines are not glued up under the bowsprit before cutting off as close as possible. Note the position of hands for this operation with the cotton trapped between fingers of the left hand, complete 'follow through' control being gained by placing the right hand hard up to the bottle neck (see Photo. No. 16).

PHOTOGRAPH No. 16

PLACING OF DECK HOUSE

Bend a wire tool to deposit a small quantity of white glue on the deck on which to place the deck house, which should now be dropped in the bottle and jiggled into position midships, alongside the hull. Your tool will do the rest – lift it up and over on to the glue, position and press down.

If you find this operation difficult, the problem can be obviated by creating a very simple tool Fig. 33: tie or tape a pin to the end of a long knitting needle and then bend the assembly to required shape. The pin, very gently pressed into the deck house, will enable you to carry it through to the deck where further gentle pressure will release the assemblage on the glue.

Take it easy! Finally, examine your model from both sides and adjust the yards parallel to each other. Tidy up sails.

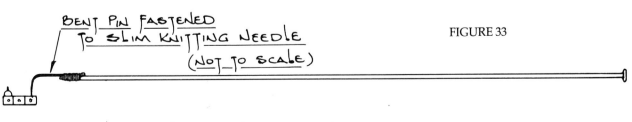

BENT PIN FASTENED TO SLIM KNITTING NEEDLE (NOT TO SCALE)

FIGURE 33

SIMPLE TOOL FOR LOCATING & FIXING DECK FITTINGS, ETC.

NECK MODEL

The author's daughter placed another mini lighthouse on rocks within the bottle neck and a neat tug-boat, cotton-wool smoke evoking a real 'atmosphere', finished off the scene. See what **you** can do. Note: thin seas will accept a glued-on model in 48 hours.

Cork and seal the bottle with red wax after one week.

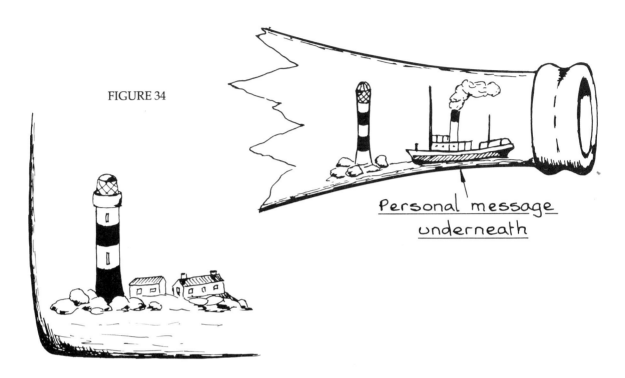

FIGURE 34

Personal message underneath

ACTUAL SIZE

FIGURE 35

A STAND for the bottle should be simple in design – two cradles joined by a dowel.

CATHERINE'S MODEL WHICH INSPIRED THE CHAPTER.

Two appropriate signal flag messages are illustrated in colour on the back cover:–

Left:– 'Splice the mainbrace' – Royal Navy.
Right:– 'We wish you a pleasant voyage' – Capt. Marryatt's 19th century merchant code.

CHAPTER 3

THREE & FOUR MASTED BARQUES

THIS MODEL is simply an extension of the 'Beginner's' the only basic difference being an extra mast and deckhouse. Note the extra mainmast hole (asterisked) (Fig. 36).

Utilising the same identical hull, proportions now begin to take on a more realistic appearance – a vessel emerging that certainly looks more interesting and workmanlike.

The addition of simulated blocks (Fig. 37), if done unobtrusively, contributes greatly to the end result and there is nothing difficult about the operation.

I recommend their inclusion before attaching the sails. Place them merely on the backstays and braces. They dry solid in about half an hour.

FIGURE 36

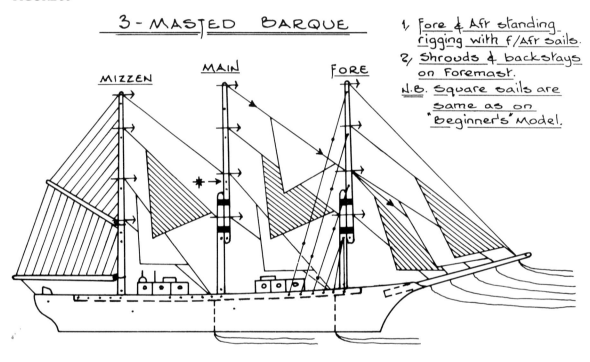

3 - MASTED BARQUE

MIZZEN   MAIN   FORE

1, Fore & Aft standing rigging with f/Aft sails.
2, Shrouds & backstays on Foremast.
N.B. Square sails are same as on 'Beginner's' Model.

FIGURE 37

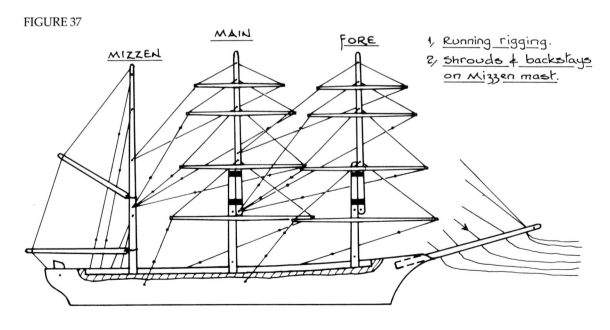

MIZZEN   MAIN   FORE

1, Running rigging.
2, Shrouds & backstays on Mizzen mast.

METHOD AND ROUTINE FOR SIMULATING BLOCKS

1. Place a small amount of white glue on a jar top, mix in very small amounts of Humbrol enamel or water colour to bring it to a dark brown shade. The result should be fairly thin so that –

2. it can be transferred to the rigging with a finely pointed cocktail stick. If you feel the need to practice first, then simply tape a cotton across the open top of a jam jar. Take up a minute quantity on the stick end and detach it with slight movement back and front of the cotton. N.B. On future models, when background experience gives you confidence to use a more delicate rigging thread, it is possible to create quite realistic blocks on the shrouds. (See 'Collector's Model'): Fig. 48.

Here then, is a test of the skills you have acquired thus far for a 'confidence booster' before going on to tackle either the 4-masted variation, the 4-masted ship or the new concept of an upright (decanter-style) S.I.B. in Chapter 5.

From this point, don't hesitate to introduce details and ideas of your own. Great satisfaction is derived when **your** built-in variations produce a finished item that is, to some extent, unique.

Everything you have read in Chaper 2, as previously stated, applies to this and all subsequent models – USE IT AS YOUR GUIDELINE ALWAYS. Memo. – don't forget to angle yards and secure braces with glue.

With your 'Beginner's Model' successfully behind you, the 3 Masted barque is really 'plain sailing'. In spite of additional 'top-hamper', your 1 litre bottle will accept the finished ship through the neck almost as readily. On this occasion, remember that you have 2 pairs of cottons coming out under the hull. Glue them in position exactly as before, severing when secure. With 2 of the 3 masts held permanently upright, 'bedding down' on your viscous glue is more easily accomplished. Again, allow ample time for setting before glueing and severing off the bowsprit lines.

By now, you will have realised the wisdom of 'duplicating' on work, especially in the creation of a 'store' of puttied bottles. Always replace them as used.

N.B. 75 centilitre bottles will normally accept these models, but always test internal height first.

PHOTOGRAPH No. 18

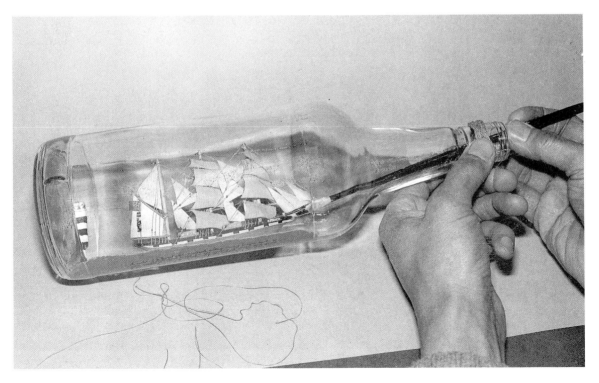

3 Masted barque – (better proportioned) Lines being removed.

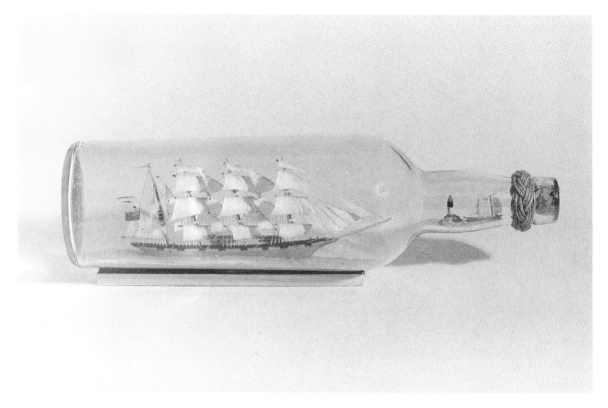

THE FOUR MASTED BARQUE
The message inside the bottle reads:
"Made by Léon Labistour (Christmas 1965) for his fiancée – Patricia Newton of Kirkella, Hull."

4 MASTED BARQUE

When you decide to make the 4 masted barque (Fig. 38), it may be possible to accommodate the slightly longer hull to a sea recess already created with the original 'dummy'. Use one of the heavier wire tools to extend the stern end of the recess – putty will often respond to firm pressure even after a few weeks drying out in the bottle.

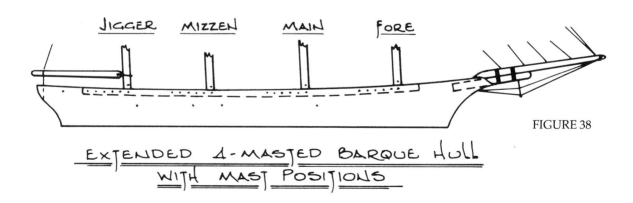

FIGURE 38

EXTENDED 4-MASTED BARQUE HULL WITH MAST POSITIONS

Jigger mast (1 part) as the 3-masted barque. Fore and aft sails used for the 3-masted barque should be 'tailored' to fit this model. Square sails are same as the 'Beginners' model.

Considerably increased 'top-hamper' certainly necessitates greater care when bottling the 4 masted barque and it would be prudent to select a bottle with adequate neck entry. Don't be afraid of slight tightness on the way in but, if unsure at any stage, bring out the ship and try another bottle.

As an extra variation, you could make a double bowsprit – i.e. a short bowsprit with jib-boom glued on top. Consult the drawing (Fig. 38) noting position of the dolphin-striker, which I always make from a mono-filament bristle as follows: cut a 1½" length at an angle to form a pointed end, insert into the drilled No. 75 hole from the top and pull through with pliers leaving about ¼" protruding. Now nip the filament with the pliers to flatten it, then draw it into the hole to leave it firmly held. Reduce the piece left to ½" – bring a small flame carefully to the end and form a small 'blob' (practice first). This 'end-stop' obviates any chance of the lines slipping off. Tuck the ends neatly away glued into a hole under the bows (see Fig. 38).

NOTE—: Mono-filament, such as used by the author, is an extremely versatile material and a 'must' for inclusion in any ship-modeller's materials box. It is delicate in appearance – strong, accepts paint, will even drill with care and, more importantly, responds to a flame by curving to a convenient davit shape! One finds many uses for it.

FIGURE 39

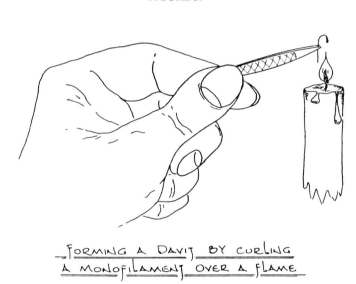

_Forming a davit by curling a monofilament over a flame

CHAPTER 4
A FOUR MASTED SHIP (Collectors Model)

FOR a really satisfying model, one to challenge your acquired skills and experience – this chapter sets before you a four-masted **ship** (i.e. square rigged on all masts) and typical of a period around 1875 – 1880. This was a rig that fell from favour, the number of four masted ships built being quite small and many that carried the rig originally were cut down to four-masted barques at a later date. Such a vessel would be steel-built and in the order of a 1,700 – 2,000 gross tonnage.

THE BOTTLE

Dimensions of the old-style Teacher whisky bottle used by the Author for this model have always been regarded as optimum and are as follows: length 14″, diameter 4″, neck entry 15/16″, liquid capacity 2½ litres. Unfortunately, this bottle is no longer manufactured having been replaced by a new design more modern in concept, but there are many other similar ones in use. Pubs and Golf clubs are particularly good 'hunting ground' and you are advised to grab at anything going. It is a fact, that until all labels are soaked off and the bottle dried out, its usability remains uncertain – the larger the bottle, the more prone it seems to distortion. Persevere in your search for good clear bottles, however – in and amongst, you will find them.

Quite often, bottles emerge with a perfect viewing side but poor rear, in which instances you would do well to consider painting a sky background inside. Simply extend the tool you have already made to put on a fairly opaque, off-white background as a 'base' for darkish clouds scumbled on, when it is almost dry. Don't worry about artistic shortcomings – the ship with its full sail covers up a lot and, besides – it is merely an atmosphere required, that will emphasise an overall 'sailor-made' appearance.

PUTTYING

Whatever the length of sea required in your bottle, make the coloured putty 'sausage' ½″ in diameter. When flattened out evenly to 1¼″ wide, it will be the correct depth for the wave-making and recess-forming routine. (At this stage, urging you to make up several bottles should not be required). With the slightly increased depth of sea, allow a bit longer time for the putty to set. In creating your dummy hull, you could omit to hollow out the deck.

NOTES ON MAKING THE HULL

We are now on to a ship of far greater dimensions and complexity, worthy of special considerations – indeed, moving 'towards better modelling'. Chapter 2 depicted an easy-to-follow hull-making routine designed, as much as anything, to get the Beginner going and, whilst the finished result was quite acceptable, visually, its sheer line must be regarded to some extent as semi-illusory. Our 'Collector's' hull, using 3/4″ x 7/8″ wood, will follow a routine to produce a more authentic appearance where the deck will rise parallel with the bulwark capping.

First create a card template of the hull profile and mark this carefully on both narrow sides of the wood with a bold outline (Fig. 40).

To remove the surplus wood (there are many ways) the modeller can use any method he wishes. The **only** one that I recommend is with a round-bottomed spokeshave which, like all cutting tools, should be kept well sharpened. This is a tool used somewhat infrequently but a little practice soon gains complete familiarity. I cannot stress too much the importance of acquiring such a tool if you haven't one already. Used properly, it not only saves time and energy in the creation of all sheer shapes, but also produces a superior result. It goes without saying that your profile outlines must coincide perfectly.

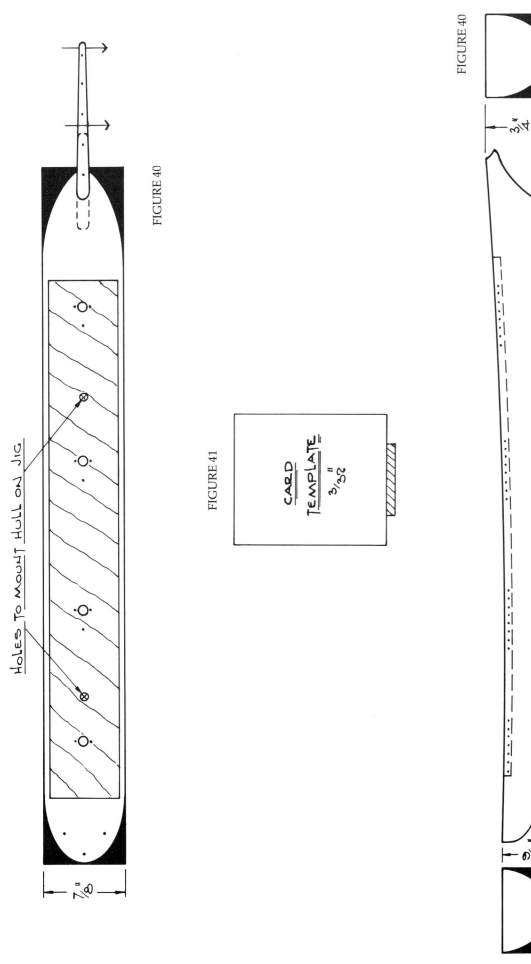

HOLES TO MOUNT HULL ON JIG

7/8"

FIGURE 40

CARD
TEMPLATE
3/32"

FIGURE 41

FIGURE 40

END TEMPLATE

3/4"

HULL PROFILE

9/16"

END TEMPLATE

FIGURE 40

35

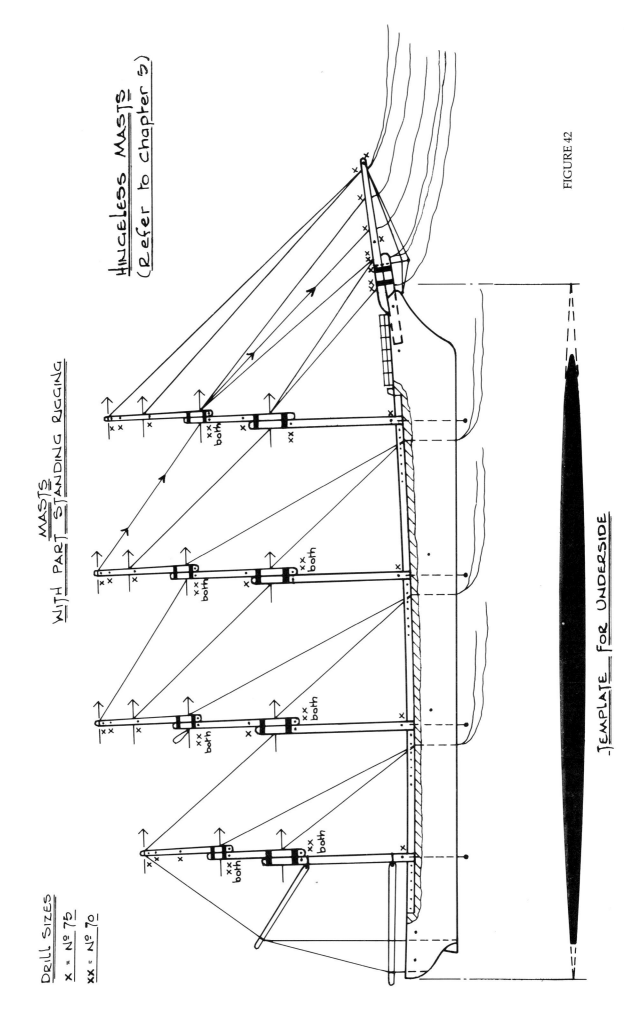

HINGELESS MASTS
(Refer to Chapter 5)

MASTS
WITH PART STANDING RIGGING

DRILL SIZES
x = N° 75
xx = N° 70

both
both
both
both
both
both

TEMPLATE FOR UNDERSIDE

FIGURE 42

At this stage, it is really essential to create a workstand (Fig. 44) for holding the model when required: With the wood held securely in the workstand, mount the assembly into a vice and remove the top surface, afterwards using a trysquare to confirm trueness of the deck level.

Now mark the curved topside as illustrated and hollow out the shaded deck area to a depth of 3/32″. To do this, make chisel cuts on the ends and **lightly** score the bulwark lines with your knife or 'scribing tool'. Once you have a groove going, gradually increase the pressure on your knife to a depth of 3/32″. A gouge is a most useful tool for initial hollowing out followed by a 3/8″ chisel for levelling off. This is not a job to be rushed – one soon realises the vulnerability of the bulwarks. Take out the central 'meat' first with the gouge, humouring the grain if necessary, but when using the chisel – angle it away from the bulwarks to avoid damage. N.B. the chisel should be used with the shaped side downwards. A simple card template is useful for measuring the depth of the hollow: (Fig. 41).

The best tools are of the home-made variety and a "scratch stock" certainly comes into this category. Basically, it is a piece of mounted, thin, hardened steel with an edge that will scrape wood surfaces and leave a flat, smooth finish. My own version is a broken-off piece of single-edged razor blade about .33mm thick, measuring 9/16″ x 3/4″. Once your deck has been roughed out, the humble scratch-stock, scraped along the surface, will quickly produce a beautiful finish. Use it either mounted or held simply in the fingers, as I do.

Now remove from the workstand and mark the ends and underside from templates as illustrated: Figs. 40 & 42. Mount on the workstand and plane off to the lines, keeping to the dotted lines on the underside. Now remove and shape round the topside curves on the ends with a knife. Mark the side profile lines at bow and stern and carve away to the required shapes.

Sandpaper the entire hull, giving careful support to the bulwarks when rubbing down the deck. Fold a light grade of sandpaper into a rounded shape to smooth off the curved cut-out into which the bowsprit hole is drilled (3/32″ drill). Glue in a bowsprit with jibboom atop, to plan size: (Fig. 42). Fine down bulwarks as instructed in Chapter 2.

Prepare the hull for marking and drilling precisely as with foregoing models.

SEQUENCE FOR DRILLING

1. Drill all No. 75 holes first, as follows: bulwarks, mast hinge holes (if you wish to use a hingeless mast technique, refer to the routine described in Chapter 5) single bollards, davits, bowsprit, flag lines on poop, etc.
2. Next use a No. 70 drill for the 6 holes that penetrate the starboard side of the hull horizontally, emerging portside.
3. Use a 1/32″ drill for vertical holes directly behind the fore, main and mizzen masts.
4. For capstans (3 in all) – make holes 3/32″ deep with 3/32″ drill.

PAINTING

The hull can now be painted to your own preference. Follow the basic 'undercoating' process outlined in Chapter 2. Decide whether you wish a smart, 'newly launched' appearance, or one where the vessel has just docked, weatherstained after a rough passage – a 'worn' effect is easily obtained by judicious patchy sandpapering through to the under-coat, and rubbing in with the fingers rust coloured and black smudgings. If you settle for a 'worn' finish to your hull, then remember the appearance of your decks, masts, yards, sails and flags should also carry through. Once the painting is complete, it is advisable to put into position as many deck-fittings as possible, keeping them always to minimum size.

Mounting the hull on the stand at this stage (see Fig. 43) is strongly to be recommended. Not only does this assist the work but also obviates a lot of undesirable handling. Stepping of the masts is made much easier, the 3 carefully drilled ½″ holes accommodating the stay-lines behind the masts through to the 'securing card'.

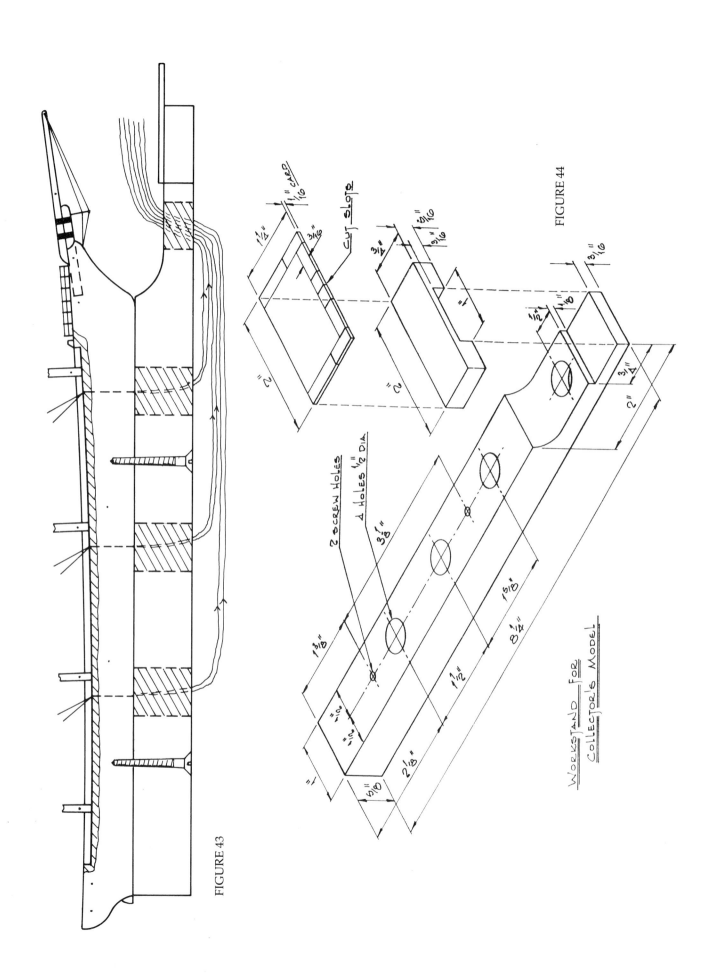

FIGURE 43

FIGURE 44

WORKSTAND FOR
COLLECTOR'S MODEL

38

DECK FITTINGS

FIGURE 45

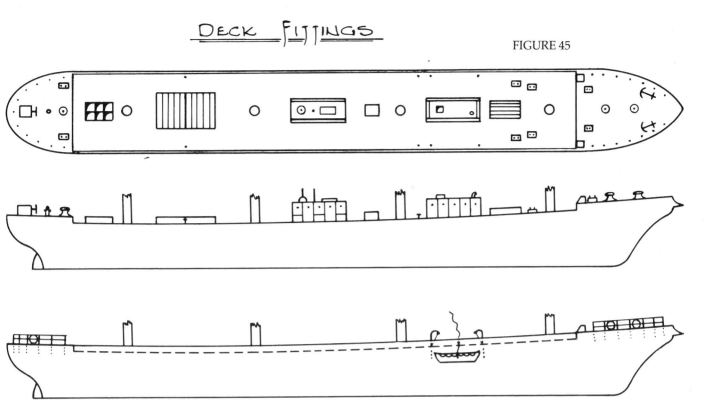

Deck details shown on the plan (Fig. 45) represent a good basic layout for your model. It can be added to considerably, of course, and the modeller with skills to fashion the multitude of 'extras' will know just how far to go.

CAPSTANS: make these on the end of cocktail sticks cut to basic shape first with a sharp knife and then rounded with a piece of folded sandpaper.

BOLLARDS: glue small rectangles of 1-ply veneer on deck and when really secure, prick and drill 2 holes to take black monofilament to represent the metal posts to which mooring ropes are secured. Single bollards can be represented by monofilament inserted in the deck, first having created a 'blob end' – (see Chap. 3).

LIGHTHOUSES: navigation lights at port and starboard should be made quite small, again on the end of cocktail sticks and glued into drilled holes.

WHEELHOUSE AND WHEEL: care and patience exercised with this tricky item can produce a feature that enhances the model more than any other. The wheelhouse is first made to plan size – paint it white, panel with pencil lines and colour appropriately. The wheel rim and spokes are then made from fine thread previously stiffened with glue (run it between finger and thumb for best result). Glue a wheel rim directly onto the end of the wheel-box, position one double-length spoke across the rim, followed by six more single length, to make up a total of 8 spokes.

BINNACLE: a delicate item but attainable with care and made on the end of a cocktail stick. Knife to shape, drill a No. 75 hole where indicated and thread in a monofilament that has a heated 'blob end'. Draw this tightly up to the binnacle side, carefully cut off the end to approx. 1/8″ and apply a flame to create a matching ball. Paint these red and green and glue into position on deck.

FIGURE 46
Deck Fittings
(illustrations enlarged)

Capstan

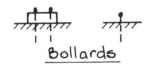
Bollards

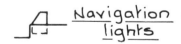
Navigation lights

Wheelhouse

Binnacle

DECK HOUSES AND HATCHES: the modeller can be left with his own ideas for style and decoration of these standard items, but keep to plan sizes.

Deck House

LIFEBOATS AND DAVITS: lifeboats are best made from good, smooth cocktail sticks – in pairs. Knife out the top curves and ends as illustrated, sand smooth and then separate. Carve and sand the other two ends. Paint and decorate as you wish but try to choose a pale shade on which looped lines may be effectively pencilled. Boats look best glued outboard with outboard-facing davits – but, you will need to check adequacy of the bottle neck entry first, otherwise, glue boats on the inner bulwark and adjust the davits correspondingly.

Lifeboat & Davits

A glued cotton gives complete security when attached to the lifeboat first via a centrally drilled hole and then inserted into a hole in the bulwark – see illustration.

ANCHORS: make from stiffened cotton (black). Carefully glue to deck.

Anchors

LIFEBELTS: these add a neat and colourful touch, though somewhat 'fiddly' to handle. Make them from stiffened white crochet cotton (about No. 60) tied and knotted around a cocktail stick. Cut off one of the tie-lines and before installation, quarter with red paint. Place 4 up for'ard and 2 on the poop rail (outboard) secured into holes exactly as the rail stanchions.

Lifebelts

FIGUREHEAD: best made and glued in position at this stage if you opt for one and perhaps not as difficult as you would imagine. Personal ingenuity comes to the fore! My own routine is to carve a basic shape on the end of a cocktail stick e.g. a ¾ length female figure, not more than 12mm in overall length.

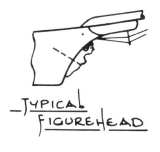

TYPICAL FIGUREHEAD

This is then drilled centrally to take a monofilament which assists handling and provides extra security when inserted into a hole under the bows.

RAILS: rails are made simply and efficiently on a jig that should take no more than 30 minutes to create (Fig. 47), the Author's own particular design being double-sided so that, provided the threads are wound on correctly, it will produce 20″ of rail at one winding. No. 100 crochet cotton is used for the upright stanchions and Gütermann 100% polyester thread for the horizontal rails. Make sure that they touch where they cross each other. Give the entire assembly a coating of French polish or watered-down P.V.A. glue applied with a brush and, when dry, remove each side from the jig and store in a jar. Fig. 46 indicates how your rail should look prior to fitting to the edges of the deck after careful cutting with a **new** blade. Install the fo'c'sle rails first: cut appropriate lengths, lay in position and lightly pencil points of the first 4 stanchions. Prick and drill to a depth of 1/16″ (No. 75 drill), slightly enlarging the holes afterwards with a sharp compass point. Glue the stanchions in, leave to dry very securely and then complete the rest. With the poop, glue in the first 3 or 4 stanchions and work round gradually. N.B. Never make rails of wire – they are vulnerable during the 'bottling process' whereas cotton rails are not only easy to create and install but will withstand the harshest treatment.

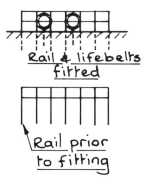

Rail & lifebelts fitted

Rail prior to fitting

FIGURE 47

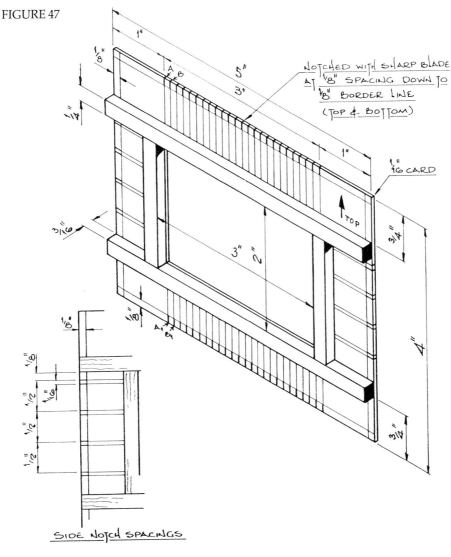

Side Notch Spacings

Jig For Rail Making

JIG FOR RAILS

MATERIALS: 1 piece stiff card 5″ x 4″ x 1/16″
2 pieces wood-strip 5″ x ¼″ x 3/16″
2 pieces wood-strip 2″ x ¼″ x 3/16″

INSTRUCTIONS

Mark card as illustrated.

Cut out 3″ x 2″ centre.

Notch the top and bottom lines with a **sharp** blade to the 1/8″ border line.

Notch the 4 pairs of lines also on the sides.

Glue the wood-strips as indicated to the board.

Begin at the point A with a knotted cotton (for anchorage) on the reverse side and wind on in one continuous length as follows:– bring the cotton down to A1 and pull into the cut slot. Return on the reverse side and pull cotton into A to emerge front side. Manipulate the line into slot B to emerge on the reverse. Bring down and pull into slot B1. You are now on the front side with your routine set for continuing.

Wind the horizontal lines similarly.

MASTS: (sequence important). Make each mast to the plan sizes (Fig. 42), in 3 sections (note that the main and mizzen masts are identical). Mark, prick and drill all arrowed holes at the 'doublings' with a No. 70 drill, No. 75 for the others. Glue the bottom parts together first, using a bristle as previously explained and add the top sections later, when quite secure. "Eye up" for straightness at all times and test each mast for strength.

Masts at this stage will lie conveniently flat for pricking and drilling the 'dot' holes. Take care to use the correct size drill for each individual hole. (See Fig. 42)

Next, wrap neat bands of masking tape around the 'doublings' where indicated, long enough for about two turns. Wires should now be cut to approx. 1½″ lengths for insertion in the hinge-holes, then neatly bent to form over-long hinges. Put each mast into position on deck and trim off any surplus hinge wire protruding from the hull's underside. Endeavour to produce a secure, yet readily removable mast.

YARDS: are attached to the masts with No. 100 crochet cotton and a new and useful technique is put forward for your consideration – one which, however, is not without its slight drawback.

Briefly, it involves tying on yards as normal and then wriggling them free to leave loops glued in position on the mast.

Stepping of masts which have been freed from the encumbrances of yards, makes the work comparatively easy. The only problem affecting this method is the possibility of breaking a loop when re-inserting the yard, which is then somewhat awkward to replace.

If you adopt this method, be sure to return each yard to its original loop. There is no reason, of course, why you should not step your masts with yards 'in situ' as before, but whichever method you opt for, do remember to angle the yard before gluing the loop-hold securely around the mast.

N.B. Always tie yards on where indicated i.e. slightly below their respective 'dot' holes. For sizes of yards – see Fig 51.

STEPPING OF MASTS – Fig. 48, "standing rigging". FACE MODEL TO THE RIGHT →

A model of this quality calls for fine, delicate rigging and a thread such as Gütermann's 100% polyester combines these qualities along with strength. Always seek neutral colours for rigging e.g. hempen shades.

With other models behind you and a complete understanding of all basic techniques, rigging this 'Collectors' item should pose no problems.

1.) Put up the Foremast, thread and knot a 24″ length of rigging line and take this through the 'arrow' hole at the mast head, thence through hole No. 1 in the jibboom and down into the central card slot. (Fig. 44)

Angle the mast correctly, then secure the line by bringing it under and up the starboard side-slot. For a 'belt and braces' job, tuck it away into the corner slot. The line is now under the card where all other jibboom lines will join it eventually, by the same route.

Proceed to rig shrouds and backstays exactly to the plan.

2.) Put the Mainmast into position, take your masthead line through the upper 'doubling' of the Foremast and then down through hole No. 3 in the jibboom. Draw the line into the central card slot, angle the Mainmast absolutely parallel with the Foremast then tuck away the loose line with the previous one.

3.) Stepping the Mizzenmast has one initial difference: the masthead line passes through the Mainmast upper 'doubling' and then down the deck hole behind the Foremast. Use tweezers to draw the needle through the jig. This line is one of 6 emerging under the hull, all of which will be brought up for'ard into the slot portside of centre – thence into the port side-slot and returning into the corner. It is good to have all lines firmly held but do make sure that the mast is parallel before rigging out shrouds etc.

4.) The Jiggermast must be put up with the gaff and boom already tied in place. Take the masthead line through the lower 'doubling' of the Mizzenmast, thence down the deck hole behind the Mainmast. Bring the line for'ard to join the previous one, first angling the mast correctly before firmly securing.

Before rigging out shrouds and backstays, the boom and gaff are held in the positions indicated by the plan, as follows: thread a 12" cotton, bring it up the stern hole and neatly glue the knotted end flush. 'Reverse loop' and glue the ends of boom and gaff, finishing off at the masthead, again with 'reverse loops' and glue.

Now complete the mast rigging.

Complete the Standing Rigging by including all other fore and aft staylines, making sure that knots are of adequate size. Note the looped (free-running) end of the line that goes through the Mizzenmast upper 'doubling'.

Before proceeding to the Running Rigging, straighten masts and 'eye up' from the stern. Satisfy yourself that they are perfectly at right angles to the deck, then put a spot of glue on both sides of each lower mast where the first 4 shroud lines penetrate. This prevents lateral movement of the masts.

It does not go amiss to make occasional tests during construction of a model, especially one of this comparative complexity. The main query remains as always: 'will the masts fold down flat and everything enter the bottle neck? If not, why not? Make a test now and at various stages of the Running Rigging.

RUNNING RIGGING (lifts and braces): (Fig. 50)

If you opted to remove yards from their loops – now return all the foremost ones, gently twisting them back into position. Glue neatly at the centre to prevent any slipping and then rig out lifts and braces. Face model to the right.

Routine is the same as for previous models. Begin by tying a threaded cotton on the bottom yardarm. Take the cotton through the mast hole indicated, back loop at the opposite end to form the lift, completing with the backbrace by penetrating through the hull (portside) and tying off on the yardarm where you started.

Rigging of the first three yards follows this same route. Complete the foremast to plan and then adopt the exact same routine for the mainmast. The first three braces on the mizzen are taken through the hole (asterisked) on the poop side. On the jigger, the first two backbraces go through the rearmost horizontal hull hole whilst the top two yards take their lines for'ard through the loop before being attached at the opposite yard end.

N.B. Keep these for'ard-facing braces tipped **over** the yardarms.

Care must be taken not to foul other lines when penetrating holes that already carry rigging.

EXTRA RIGGING: (optional)

Limiting factors operate to such an extent when rigging a Ship for a bottle that the merest suggestion of detail is really all that is permitted. On occasions, the Modeller must make up his own mind where to draw the line, a point often determined by personal skills, ingenuity and fineness of material.

The economic theory of 'diminishing returns' comes to mind when considering further additions to a model. Do they actually contribute to overall effect? In the case of extra 'elaboration' of the 2nd and 3rd braces (see Fig. 50), I think the answer must be affirmative. By a simple technique, a large open area is effectively filled in – which must be good.

Simply thread a cotton, tie the end where indicated (starboard side) with a knot and take the needle through the 'doubling hole'. On the port side, the line is then tied on similarly – perhaps slightly lower, which then allows tautening afterwards by sliding the knot upwards. All the knots when finally glued into position will form part of the simulated blocks overall.

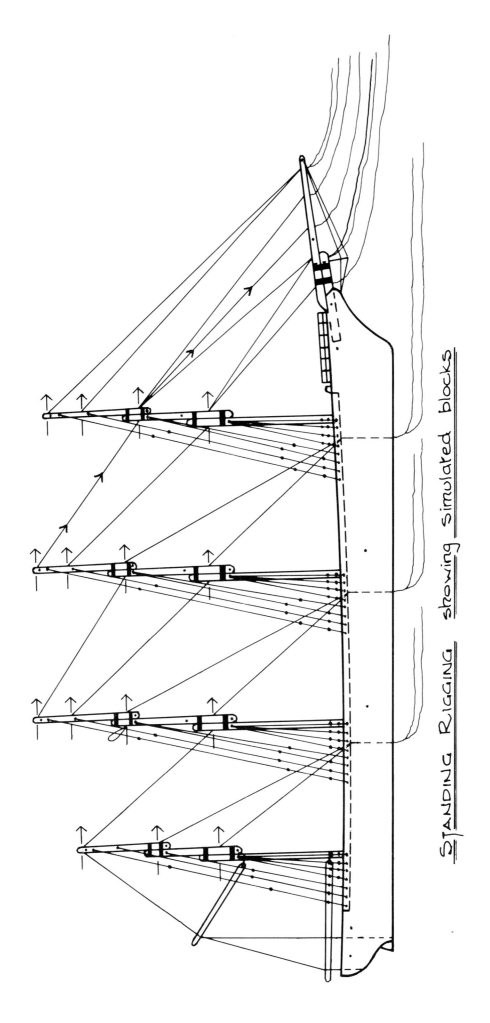

STANDING RIGGING showing simulated blocks

FIGURE 48

44

BLOCKS:

Simulated blocks and dead-eyes are created at this stage before putting up the sails. Refer to Chapter 3 for method and Fig. 50 for details. It is important to use a very finely pointed cocktail stick.

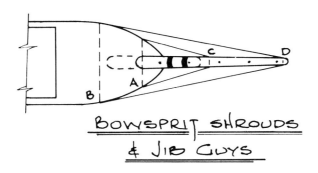

BOWSPRIT SHROUDS
& JIB GUYS

FIGURE 49

Having rigged out the dolphin striker in the same manner as the 4 masted barque, the bowsprit shroud arrangement (Fig. 49) is created as follows: thread a 20″ cotton and take it through hole A, leaving a small end trailing, thence through C. and back again through A. to emerge port side. Withdraw the lines slightly, apply glue and tauten to secure. Follow the same routine through B, D, to complete. Sever the four trailing ends when the glue has dried.

SAILS:

Cut all the sails to plan (Figs. 52 and 54), square sails slightly deeper (see Chapter 2); 'belly' them and glue in position. Take care with the staysail marked with an asterisk – position it so that it does not prevent the mizzen mast from collapsing fully. After the spanker has been set up, put in the flag line. Neatly tie a cotton at the gaff tip and take the two ends through the deck holes, glued in taut. Always attempt to include an authentic message with signal flags.

ANGLING YARDS AND SECURING BRACES:

All yards on masts can be held to correct angles (excepting the topmost one on the fore, main and mizzen masts) by gluing braces appropriately, as before, in the 'Beginners' chapter. It is not a terribly difficult operation to manoeuvre and adjust these 3 exceptions, after bottling.

N.B. Braces on the 2 top yards of the jigger mast are secured with a spot of glue where they touch the loop.

BOTTLING:

Care, caution, patience and thought at this stage goes without saying. Time taken now to ensure the model's safe passage through the bottle neck always pays off. Indeed, the modeller with any qualms might even consider a "dummy run" – i.e. actually collapsing the masts and preparing the ship as for insertion, then bringing everything up again outside the bottle. This literally gives one some insight as to what happens after 'launching' and the action subsequently required.

Re-reading the complete text in Chapter 2 under 'Bottling' cannot be too highly recommended before progressing further. The basic principles are exactly the same.

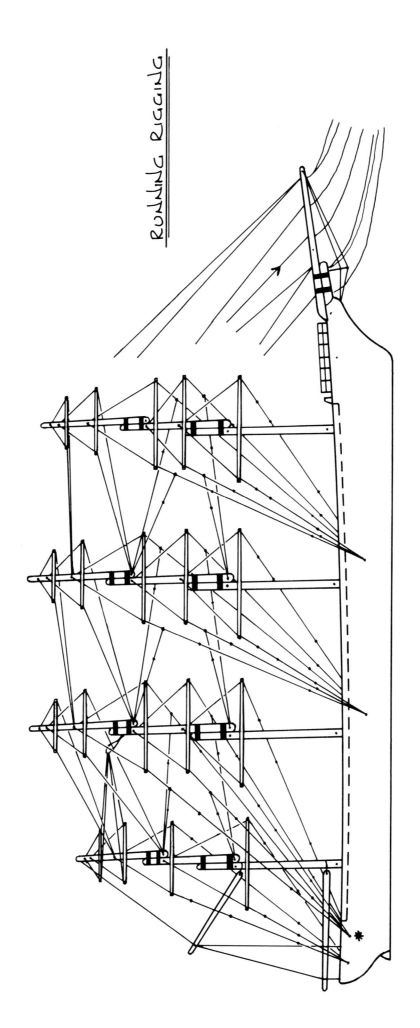

FIGURE 50

46

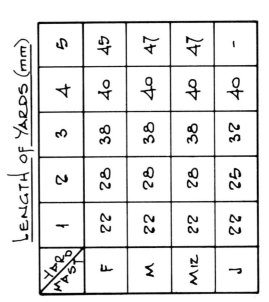

LENGTH OF YARDS (mm)

YARD \ MAST	1	2	3	4	5
F	22	28	38	40	45
M	22	28	38	40	47
MIZ	22	28	38	40	47
J	22	25	32	40	-

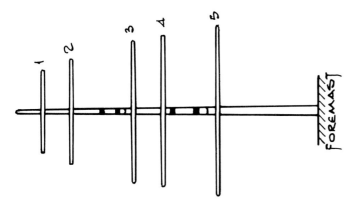

FOREMAST

MAIN & MIZZEN

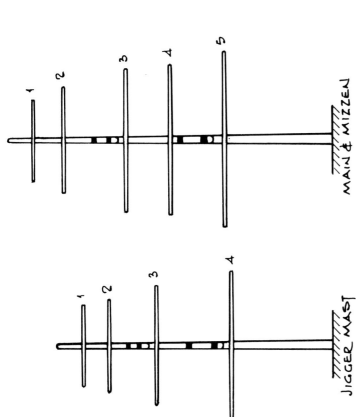

JIGGER MAST

FIGURE 51

'BEDDING' THE SHIP:

With the ship in its fully erect state inside the bottle and the 6 cottons emerging under the hull severed (using the technique described in Chapter 2), we are now ready for glueing it down into the sea's recess.

To obviate reiteration of the same instructions for the 'bedding' process, removal of bowsprit lines, placing of deck-houses, etc. given in Chapter 2, the modeller's attention is drawn thereto.

N.B. Check that the putty sea has hardened sufficiently.

HINGELESS MASTS

Reference to Chapter 5 will draw your attention to the possible need for some slight individual attention to the foremast from your bent knitting needle on erection in the bottle i.e. the base of the mast may require a gentle, encouraging push into the deck indentation.

NECK MODEL

Here is an opportunity to design and create your own (rigged) neck model to impart an individualistic finishing touch.

The funnel of a tug-boat can bear the modeller's initials on the coloured band. Addition of cotton-wool smoke, delicately 'teased out' and smudged with graphite scraped off a pencil lead gives an authentic touch. The funnel is inserted into a pre-prepared hole on the deck house, with a pair of tweezers once the hull is settled in position in the bottle neck.

Pilot schooners, tug boats, and paddle steamers are all suitable, or you may prefer a small scene with a lighthouse.

COLLECTOR'S NECK MODELS

FIGURE 53

BRITISH LIGHTSHIPS ARE
ALWAYS PAINTED RED

48

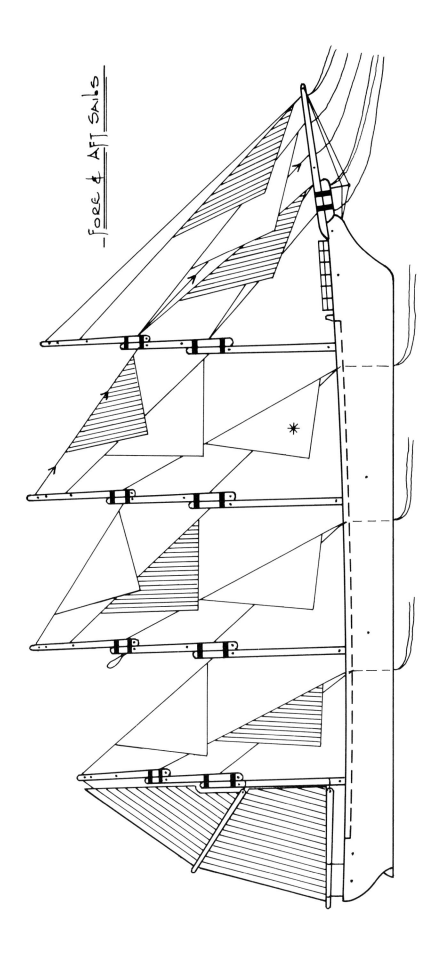

FORE & AFT SAILS

FIGURE 52

49

FIGURE 54

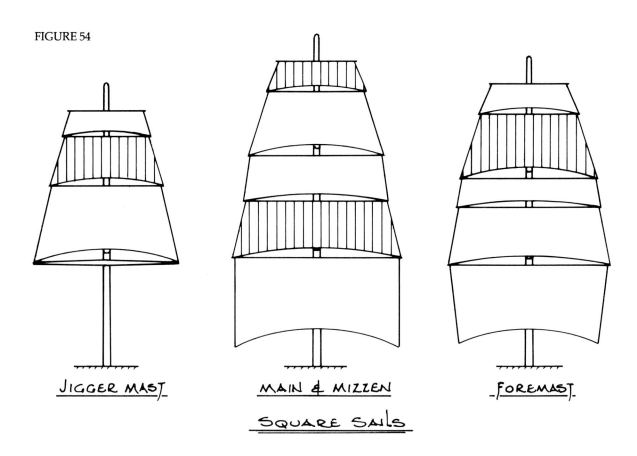

JIGGER MAST   MAIN & MIZZEN   FOREMAST

SQUARE SAILS

PHOTOGRAPH No. 20

'Collectors' Model ready for 'bottling'

50

CHAPTER 5

THE UPRIGHT (DECANTER-STYLE) MODEL

THE AUTHOR'S own introduction to this particular style of S.I.B. came about influenced by a variety of factors, completion of the very first model resulting in a sudden and dramatic uplift of standards.

Initially, a friend had persuaded me to enter something for The British Handicrafts Competition back in the mid-fifties and, with naive enthusiasm, I set my sights on the coveted Silver Medal! The entry, I decided, would need to display not only good workmanship but a certain degree of 'gimmicky' concept – also complete disguise of the traditional manner in which a S.I.B. was erected in the bottle i.e. with cottons passed through the bowsprit, each glued individually and severed afterwards. Any judge worth his salt would immediately look for the tell-tale points, one of the criteria being a neat finish.

The model I chose to make, in an antique decanter, was inspired by McNarry's astonishing book 'Shipbuilding in Miniature'. It was a 12 gun brig of war – though I hasten to add, with not the merest pretension towards comparison with his work. It did, however, exhibit much more ambitious detail than former models – lower and topmast shrouds with ratlines for example, also the requisite number of guns on deck lined up with their open ports, lids raised outboard. A long, highly-raked jibboom presented the judge with a clear view of its underside – if he was bothering to look! **There were no tell-tale points** – these 'give-away' features obviated by a method I had devised: viz. all cottons were taken through a centrally-drilled hole down the jibbooms length, glued and neatly severed off together. A neat blob of white coloured glue finished off the jibboom end perfectly. (See Fig. 60)

ROUTINE FOR HINGELESS MASTS

Further to this important aspect of disguising methods and technique, it was also essential to display masts stepped into deck-holes with no visible means of hingeing. The perfect answer, like a good tune, was a simple one.

At the deck positions where the masts stood, a slight indentation (approx. 1/32" deep) was made with an appropriate size drill and a No. 70 hole then drilled vertically in the centre of each indentation to emerge under the hull.

The masts were then stepped in the usual manner, but held in their respective indentations by a standard cotton glued into the base of each mast which was taken down through the deck-hole. During the rigging process, the emerging cotton under the hull was held temporarily taut with a piece of masking-tape.

Establishing these cottons is a mere 5 minutes work: prick a 'pilot hole' centrally in the base of each mast with a compass point – drill in approx. 1/16" (No. 75 drill), then carefully enlarge the hole with the same compass point. Fill the hole with glue using the point of a cocktail stick and then neatly 'bed' in the end of a long cotton. Put aside and allow PLENTY of time for the glue to set.

Very carefully sanding off the sharp edge of the mast base (the merest bit) creates a sort of 'knuckle joint' connection with the deck indentation.

When ready for the stepping process, the long cotton is needle-threaded and taken through the deck hole, held taut as suggested above.

After stepping of the masts, a small block is then established on the cottons under the hull exactly 3/32" from the base of the hull where they emerge. (See Fig. 42) These blocks prevent the masts from 'wandering' on deck during the bottling process whilst at the same time allowing them to collapse fully. Cut the surplus cotton away just below the block, when it is set hard.

The whole routine, in effect, creates a judge's dilemma – that is, one who knows what he's about. He is confronted with a model that shows no lines penetrating through the bowsprit AND, displays no visible means of hingeing! This method can be used on all models, but please note that fore-masts may sometimes require slight individual attention from your bent knitting-needle on erection in the bottle (i.e. the base of the mast may need a gentle encouraging push into the deck indentation).

For the moment, however, the modeller would do well to create his first 'decanter-style' model in as straight-forward a manner as possible, i.e. with wire hinges and one part bowsprit.

THE BOTTLE

Those listed under Materials are very suitable, this type invariably having a wider and generously accommodating neck entry, thereby permitting creation of a better-pro-portioned hull.

Make your 'dummy' first from either 5/8" x 1/2" (or 1/2" x 1/2") depending on the diameter of your bottle neck. Note the different bow shape into which a 'cutwater' is inserted, made from 1mm ply. Glue this into a groove carefully sawn with a small hack-saw blade. A rudder can be fitted similarly.

Bottles vary in internal dimension so it is important to accurately determine the overall length (boom tip to jibboom tip) to make your ship **after** puttying – i.e. by trial and error with a loose cocktail stick in the bowsprit hole.

PUTTYING

If you have placed a message within the bottle, wait until it is quite dry before dropping small 'sausages' of coloured putty centrally on the bottle base. Flatten these to an overall even depth, working carefully outwards to finish off neatly around the perimeter. (This was one further occasion when the same good friend devised the perfect tool for me – see Tools and Materials). Creating the waves should not present any problems – your existing tools will bend to shapes required. Lay on a thin coating of white paint streaked with black and then form waves. Make sure that your bottle is positioned correctly with the seams to the side. If the bottle has a 'window' (e.g. Pusser Rum and Chivas Regal) set the model facing right so that it is nicely framed within the outline. Pusser bottles are eminently suitable for upright models as the design incorporates an attractive moulded anchor. When 'bedding' the dummy hull, remember to first make a locating groove in the sea. Having pressed it down into position, a sharp upward pull under the bowsprit will remove it to leave a recess for the completed model, with perhaps a minimum of tidying if your putty was of correct consistency.

CHOICE OF SHIP

The Collier Brig chosen for your upright bottle is a model that will 'double up' for a variety of short barrel horizontal bottles e.g. House of Lords, Haig Dimple, etc. (See Photos 24 and 25).

THE HULL

This can be made from standard 1/2" x 1/2" wood or 5/8" x 1/2" if the width of the bottle neck will accept it.

Being of such small size, the sheer shape can be marked on the sides and knifed off in the hand. Chisel work to create the deck recess can be performed with the hull held in your vice, or simply sandwiched on the bench as described in Chapter 2.

Note the new bow section. Glue the 1mm ply 'cutwater' into a carefully sawn groove. It helps start the hack-saw blade if you knife a fine line first. At the stern, fit a rudder similarly or, you may test your skill and carve one as an integral part of the hull. Insert a one-part bowsprit as per plan, determining its exact length by reference to the dummy hull: (Fig. 55).

COLLIER BRIG

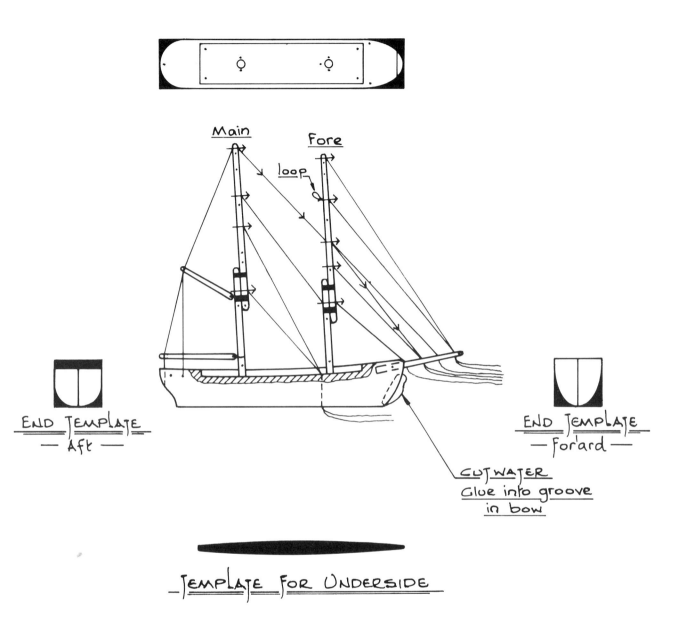

Main

Fore

loop

END TEMPLATE
— Aft —

END TEMPLATE
— for'ard —

CUTWATER
Glue into groove
in bow

TEMPLATE FOR UNDERSIDE

FIGURE 55

MASTS, YARDS AND STEPPING

Likewise, this is straightforward routine – but do refer to the plan at all times. Note the inclusion of a loop into which the braces on mainmast yards 3 and 4 are brought forward. Make this loop by tying a cotton round a 1/8" dowel, glueing the knot before neatly cutting off the loose end: (Fig. 55).

N.B. this loop runs freely back from its drilled hole.

Before stepping masts, it's a good idea to put into position as many deck details as possible. Assuming you have used ½" square wood for your hull you might like to consider mounting lifeboats outboard. See Chapter 4 for method. Davits are also best placed on deck at this stage, glued into holes where indicated facing either in or outboard.

Following stepping of the masts, employ the method suggested under 'Lifts and Braces' (Chapter 2) for preventing lateral movement.

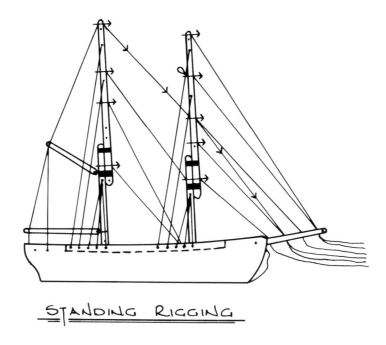

STANDING RIGGING

FIGURE 56

RUNNING RIGGING

Rig out the lifts and braces exactly to plan. Take especial care with those on main masts yards 3 and 4: after each lift has been 'back-looped' on the port side, bring your needle then through the loop and tie off at the yard end where you started.

N.B. Keep these for'ard-facing braces tipped **over** the yardarms.

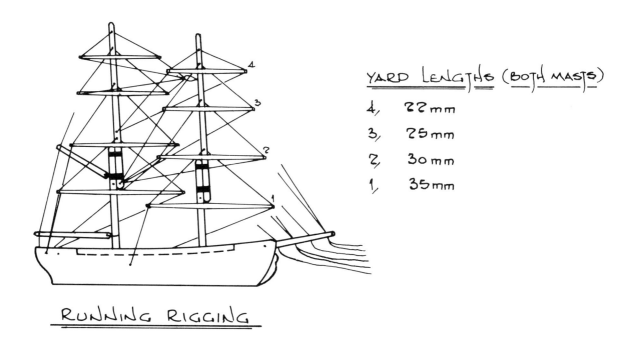

RUNNING RIGGING

YARD LENGTHS (BOTH MASTS)

4, 22 mm

3, 25 mm

2, 30 mm

1, 35 mm

FIGURE 57

BLOCKS

Form simulated blocks on shrouds, backstays and braces as described in Chapter 3, stand the model carefully aside for them to harden, before proceeding to attach sails.

SAILS

Sequence is still all-important and reference to Chapter 2 would not go amiss.

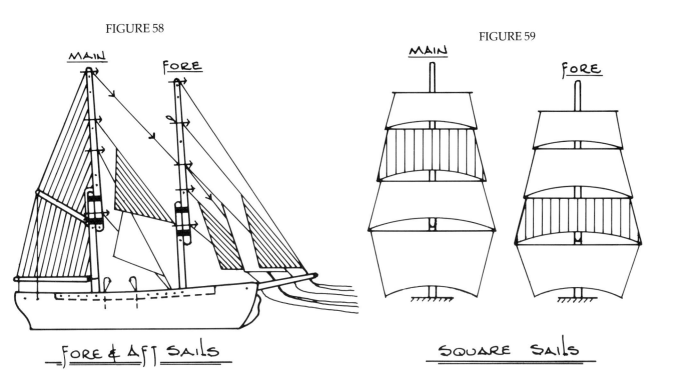

FIGURE 58   FIGURE 59

FORE & AFT SAILS   SQUARE SAILS

ANGLING YARDS AND SECURING BRACES

Set correct angle for the yards and glue braces where they penetrate the hull or mainmast. Braces that pass through the loop on the foremast are secured where they touch with a spot of glue.

FLAG LINE

When establishing your flag line, the routine to follow is exactly the same as on the 'Beginner's' model. Make sure, however, that the lines on both sides of the hull sit inside the back-braces from yards 1 and 2 on the mainmast, and that the flag line is as vertical as possible.

BOTTLING

Always examine your model carefully before bottling to ensure that everything is 'ship-shape'. Throughout making, you should have been testing occasionally for collapse of the masts – also, that lift lines run freely.

Now, providing that the sea is sufficiently hard, you may proceed with folding down the masts and the actual bottling. During insertion of the collapsed model, try bringing the masts up again whenever possible in the early stages, if only slightly – also squaring the yards. See Author's use of fingers (left hand) to hold cottons – Photo. No. 15 (Chapter 2).

Having let the ship down to the bottom of the bottle, you may experience some tendency for it to slide around when manipulating with tools. Exercise a little more perseverance, take your time and it will all come right. The routine to follow is again laid out precisely in Chapter 2, re-reading of which will remind you **now** how to conveniently 'lose' the two lines under the hull.

With the 'Upright' model, the bowsprit lines will also be glued in and removed **before** 'bedding' the ship.

This is a comparatively simple operation as the entire ship can be drawn up to the bottle neck and the lines severed at close proximity. I personally find the entire operation of bottling and completion of this type of model far easier than others.

SECURING AND REMOVAL OF BOWSPRIT LINES

Each individual modeller will, no doubt, develop his own method for this operation but the one I use for standard production is as follows:

First make sure that the model is 'tidy', then withdraw the 2 foremost lines together about 3/16" – smear on glue and draw back again. The secret of success is in holding these 2 lines taut until they can be released and left for an hour to thoroughly set. Once that is achieved, the remaining lines can be glued in position without problem, left for a further hour and the entire set then severed.

My own method of holding the 2 for'ard lines is as illustrated (Photo. No. 21) for about 3 to 4 minutes. It works, but beware of putting undue pressure on the bowsprit.

PHOTOGRAPH No. 21

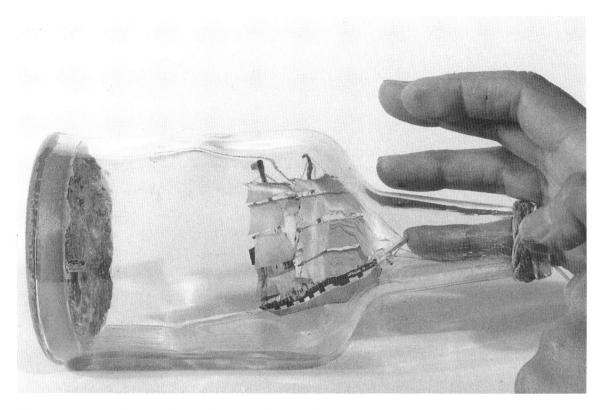

When severing lines – draw the model up to the neck and adopt a technique that gives 'follow through' control. (Photo. No. 16)

"BEDDING THE SHIP"

Place your model carefully to one side of the bottle before spreading thick glue in the sea's recess. The ship is now suspended on a suitable, slightly bent tool and deposited into position on the glue giving it a gentle but firm push down from the deck at the same time. Make sure that the ship is perfectly upright before leaving it to set firmly. At this stage, don't worry about small amounts of glue that may ooze out under the hull – they will remove or flatten later. Likewise, leave tidying of sails and yards until the hull is held rigidly in the sea.

If your model was bottled without the deck-house in position, now is the time to establish it.

As a matter of interest only, the 'competition' method of taking jib-lines through the centre of the jibboom (mentioned earlier) is briefly as follows:– a cotton is threaded down the centrally-drilled jibboom and then, starting from for'ard, a loop is drawn up out of a jib-line hole that has been drilled only half way – not penetrating through. To this loop, the jib line is glued and then drawn back through – the other lines following in turn by this same method: (Fig. 60).

FIGURE 60

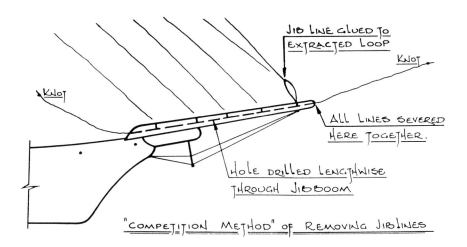

JIB LINE GLUED TO
EXTRACTED LOOP

KNOT

KNOT

ALL LINES SEVERED
HERE TOGETHER.

HOLE DRILLED LENGTHWISE
THROUGH JIBBOOM

"COMPETITION METHOD" OF REMOVING JIBLINES

The whole sequence is difficult and requires great patience and perseverance – definitely not for the inexperienced.

Incidentally, if you are wondering what happened at the British Handicrafts Competition – don't ask!

PHOTOGRAPH No. 22

CHAPTER 6
THE CLIPPER SHIP IN A HAIG DIMPLE BOTTLE

THIS BOOK would hardly be complete without inclusion of the Clipper Ship, a vessel of incomparable beauty whose entire design produced the desired effect – speed. Credit for the 'Clipper' must certainly go to American ship builders. Around the second decade of the 19th century, those in the Chesapeake Bay area began to produce fast vessels for the more profitable world trades – known as 'Baltimore Clippers'. They are not now regarded, however, as true Clippers – 'first off the stocks' is generally accepted to have been the 'Rainbow' built in 1845 at New York. Nevertheless, Baltimore Clippers, built mainly in Virginia and Maryland, had the basic concept of design form from which the true Clipper evolved.

Donald McKay, the greatest builder of American Clipper ships ('Lightning', 'Flying Fish', 'Flying Cloud', etc.) finally produced the optimum design – a vessel with fine lines and lightened hull that reduced the 'wetted' area and increased speed, concave bows and masts carrying a vast area of sail. His 'Sovereign of the Seas' created long-standing records, one passage from New York to Liverpool taking a mere 13 days 14 hours, at times attaining speeds of up to 22 knots.

Little need be said about construction of our model: the following points should be borne in mind, however.

1. Puttying is made easier with a fairly robust tool, say a heavy metal knitting needle or length of pig-wire bent to a shape that will reach all parts of the bottle. Mine is a curious looking instrument, but effective, especially in the creation of waves. Use your original

FIGURE 61

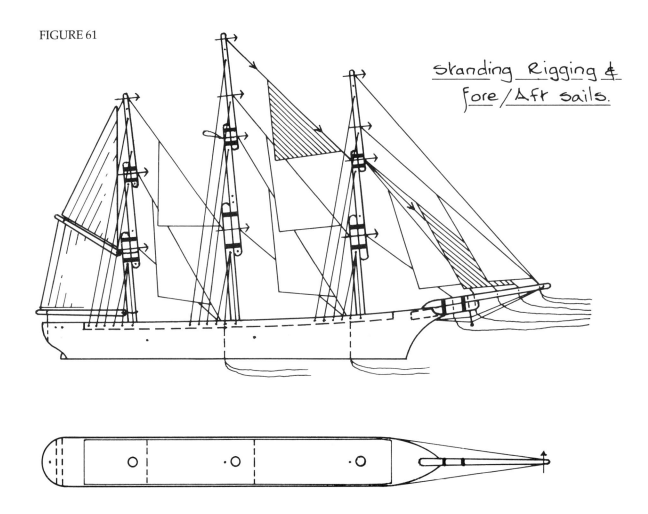

Standing Rigging & fore/Aft sails.

dummy hull for making the central recess – build the ends up neatly and artistically and on removal, increase the groove length about 1/8''.

2. The wider your hull, the better will be the proportions over all. Attempt what you can, even 1/16'' extra.

3. On this occasion, you are working at very close quarters in a bottle that can prove a bit awkward. There will be, for example, a tendency for the whole ship to slide down each side of the groove. Now you will begin to realise the benefit of a hardened putty sea (see opening remarks in 'Beginner's Chapter). My advice is to 'take it easy'. Square off yards and tauten lines even as the ship is lying down, making constant and careful observation. Glue in the hull lines (two sets of 2) and remove before the 'bedding' operation. You may find a long pair of tweezers useful for lifting the ship into the recess. Removal of bowsprit lines at such close proximity is simplicity itself.

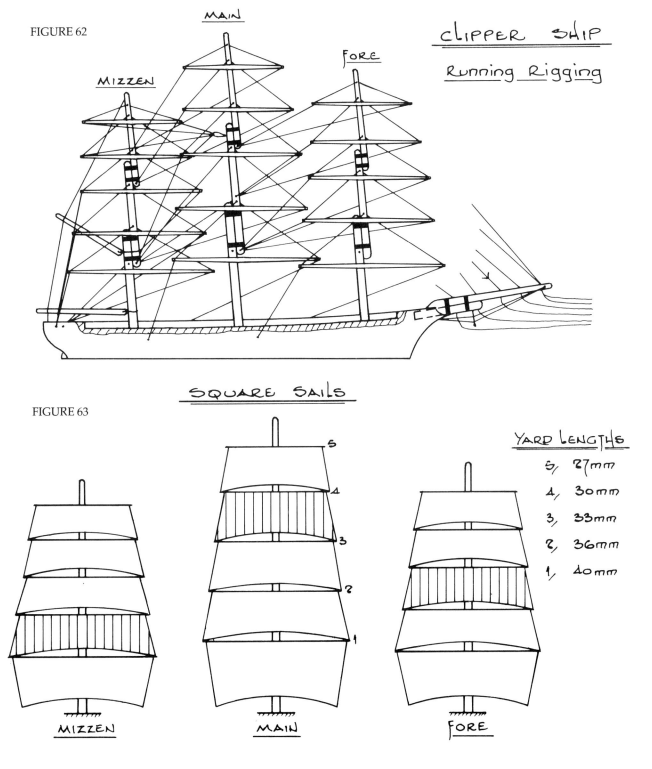

FIGURE 62

CLIPPER SHIP
Running Rigging

MAIN
MIZZEN
FORE

FIGURE 63

SQUARE SAILS

YARD LENGTHS

5,	27mm
4,	30mm
3,	33mm
2,	36mm
1,	40mm

MIZZEN MAIN FORE

THE COMPLETED CLIPPER

CHAPTER 7

THE TURK'S HEAD KNOT

A TURK'S HEAD KNOT is very easy to make on a bottle neck and yet, paradoxically, difficult to explain easily with words and diagrams. In answering queries about this very attractive knot, I have to admit referring some enquirers to local library shelves. The quick way, however, is to find some one who can show you – it takes five minutes, and once shown, never forgotten.

FIGURE 64

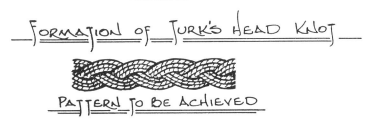

Formation of Turk's Head Knot

Pattern to be Achieved

My own routine is as follows:–

Face the bottle neck to the right, on the edge of the work table.

1. Thread a curved sacking needle with a 48″ length of hemp twine, 3/32″ diam. Hold about 5″ of the long end in the left hand and wind the threaded end over the bottle neck, crossing over, and leaving a short tail as shown in Fig. 1.

2. Take the needle as depicted in Fig. 2. under the right hand line. N.B. You should have two parallel lines running round the back of the bottle.

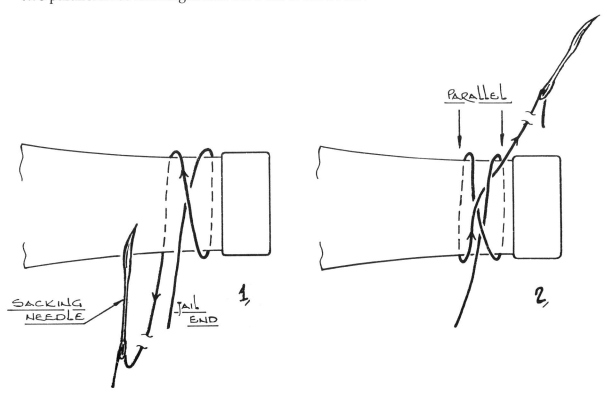

SACKING NEEDLE

TAIL END

1.

PARALLEL

2.

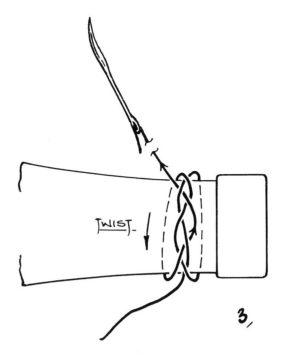

3. Twist the knot slightly towards you, and away under the bottle, so that the parallels emerge on top. Lift the left hand parallel line over the right – pick up the **new** left hand line and slip the needle under and through.

4. Twist the knot further under the bottle; now lift the right hand parallel line over the left, pick up the new right hand line and slip the needle under and through.

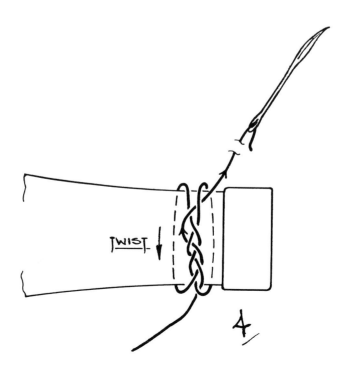

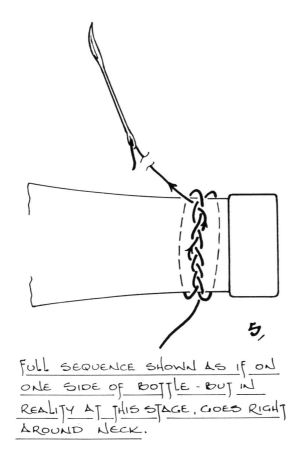

FULL SEQUENCE SHOWN AS IF ON
ONE SIDE OF BOTTLE - BUT IN
REALITY AT THIS STAGE, GOES RIGHT
AROUND NECK.

5. Finally, lift the left hand parallel line over the right, insert the needle under the new left hand line and pull through. Correct and comfortable tension in the knot at this stage is the secret of a successful outcome.

6. To complete the three part 'plait', face the bottle neck away from you, trap the tail end between the first two fingers, and, keeping the needle below the tail end, follow the line round.

*Finally, withdraw both ends slightly, insert glue, tighten and trim close.

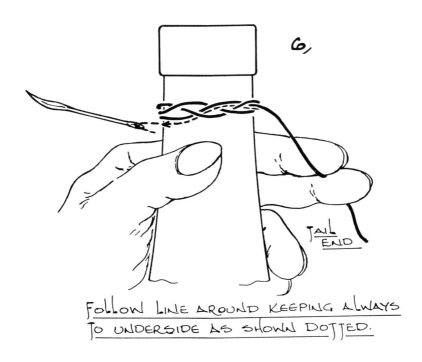

FOLLOW LINE AROUND KEEPING ALWAYS
TO UNDERSIDE AS SHOWN DOTTED.

63

COLLIER BRIG IN A 'HOUSE OF LORDS' WHISKY BOTTLE

PHOTOGRAPH No. 25

COLLIER BRIG IN A 'HAIG DIMPLE' BOTTLE

CHAPTER 8
ALTERNATIVE MODELLING

THERE is no reason why all models described in this book should not be presented in other ways and forms. 'Ringing the changes' on presentation will produce items to both complement your ships in bottles and add variety to your collection.

Models with a story or talking-point always contribute as 'conversation pieces'.

1. **'PARMA' IN A CASE.** (Photo No. 26) (using standard 4MB hull)

'Parma' in a case was created to commemorate her arrival in Hull in 1933. She was towed down river by the tug 'Seaman' (United Towing Company) of which my father-in-law was a director. The model was made for his 80th birthday, likewise the half model.

Construction of the base frame, the surrounding glass and method of securing all parts left much to be desired (I am no carpenter), but it remains to this day, perfectly whole and presentable after many years of handling. I am sure that the average modeller will have good ideas of his own but **my** basic design is set out, for what it is worth:

The stained and polished base is merely 1″ inbevelled ramin picture frame moulding, mitred the wrong way on to form a recess on which to glue down a 3/16″ thick panel of wood carrying the sea atop. As a picture framer myself, I would recommend that you take your moulding along to the framer in your locality who can machine-mitre to size in seconds and if he has an 'underpinner', get him to join up the 4 pieces – another quick job.

The panel should be cut to the size of the rebate allowing for space all round to accept the glass top – a tight fit, in fact. Prepare the surface of the wood with an undercoat and two coats of gloss paint. When dry, this will accept a putty sea and prevent absorption of any linseed oil content into the wood. Glue in position, secured with a few small pins before moulding on the sea.

There is no mystery to cutting glass but make sure your tool contains new wheels. Cut the 4 sides accurately, marking with a set-square and felt pen. Place them around the sea panel, ensuring a good fit. Brown gum-strip paper (½″ wide) is then used to join the edges outside. (An extra pair of hands can be useful). Neatly fold the gum-strip so that only ¼″ overlaps then apply the same treatment to the inside using 3/8″ wide strip. The strength imparted overall is really quite remarkable. Lastly, cut and attach a top.

'Parma's' glass cover was finally edged outside with fine veneer strips, mitred at joining places. With the ship and 'extras' neatly arranged on the hardened sea, the glass case was bedded on white PVA glue.

PHOTOGRAPH No. 26

2. COLLIER BRIG IN A RECESSED FRAME (Photo. No. 27)

All the book's models lend to this particular form of presentation and I call them 'sell-on-sight' items – more often than not, sold before chance of even hanging them on my Studio wall!

Into the rebate of a chosen frame is set another batten frame. This inner frame should be kept to a minimum depth, thereby avoiding standing the finished item too far off the wall. Optimum dimensions for the Collier Brig (upright) model are as follows:–

frame – 1″ wide approx. with rebate 8″ x 4¼″.

batten – made from 1″ x ¼″ woodstrip.

Mitre the batten frame to fit snugly inside the main frame's rebate.

N.B. use the picture frame as a jig whilst you glue the batten sides together, using a strong rubber band right round. When set firmly, remove and cut a piece of strong cardboard to size, to glue and pin on as backing. The entire interior of the 'box' should now receive flatting and painting treatment (white).

With glass in the frame, offer up the batten box to confirm a good fit and to give an idea of depth of sea required. The putty sea should literally reflect the type of sky you opt for as background, which should also be painted on the remaining sides.

Before setting up your ship on the sea, angle yards to the maximum possible before taping the glass on. It is then perfectly adequate to neatly join the two components, again with masking tape. Attach screw-eyes and hanging cord appropriately.

PHOTOGRAPH No. 27

3. A HALF MODEL IN A PICTURE FRAME

All models lend to this treatment and the adapted 'Collector's' (Photo 29) shows how attractive the finished item can be. It is virtually a ship split down the centre line, glued to a backing board and set in a recessed frame.

As with the Collier Brig in a recessed frame, strong cardboard should be used as backing to the batten frame. Cut two pieces exactly to size, one of which will be used for a final neat backing when the model is completed. The second, 'working' piece should be attached to the batten and all sides prepared by undercoating with two coats of flatting and one of gloss, after which a simple and attractive sky may be painted using oil based paint – remember to blend round into the batten sides. An alternative to painting is to glue on an appropriate sky print – overlapping three sides of the batten frame. Take care, however, not to allow the paper to soak up linseed oil from the putty.

Sequence of work should be thought out carefully by each individual modeller.

Refer to the making of half-hulls in the 'Hints and Tips' chapter. All shrouds and backstays should be glued to the bulwark in pairs before the half hull is secured to the backboard surround by a putty sea. Later, each line will be needle threaded and taken through the appropriate hole in the half masts and held on the reverse side with tape.

Once the masts have been firmly glued to the painted background drill the holes, which can all be generously oversize to facilitate all rigging. Establishing the fore-and-aft rigging, using extra long threads, and 'sewing' through the background, is relatively fast and simple. Secure with small pieces of tape on the back until all rigging is complete, when they may be finally glued.

Complete the standing rigging by threading up the shrouds and backstays.

You may now prefer to put up staysails before the yards are glued in. Ideally, yards are best made from the fibrous natured medical applicator sticks. Prick holes in the appropriate places, just for'ard of each mast and set and glue the yards in at an angle. To some extent

PHOTOGRAPH No. 28

there will be a certain amount of adjustment. Setting a ruler across the batten frame, check that the lower yards will not 'foul' the glass on completion.

Complete the running rigging – this adapts easily from the 'Collector's' model plan – then 'tailor' each square sail and neatly glue to the yards and background.

Finally add deck fittings, flags, and any scenic details. As with the Collier Brig, the batten frame can be taped to the surrounding frame and prepared for hanging.

A fully descriptive hand written panel should adorn the back, describing the ship and denoting the maker's name, etc.

PHOTOGRAPH No. 29

The completed Collector's Half Model in a picture frame.

4. FURTHER SUGGESTIONS FOR PRESENTING MODELS:–

a) Upright bottles convert into attractive table lamps. Use a 'Bottlelite' fitting and a small, plain shade.

b) Domes are available at craft shops and florists, and lend scope for various ways of presentation.

FIGURE 65

FIGURE 66

c) Mini bottles house a collection of detailed neck models.

FIGURE 67

  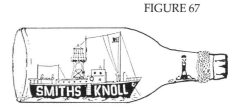

d) 'Parade of Sail' – a collection of models in a batten frame, which can also illustrate the evolution of shipping.

FIGURE 68

CHAPTER 9

MACHINE METHODS

IN THIS modern age, resort can be made to various machines in the pursuit of faster and easier progress on some routine jobs – the more obvious ones being ROUTING out of decks, and drilling. For the latter operation, I use a FLEXIBLE SHAFT mounted to an old washer motor but, on occasions, I may use a modern electric HAND DRILL that will close down to accept drills as small as No. 75. With regard to routing, however, strong emphasis must be placed on the need for extreme care. It should only be attempted after instruction from a competent wood-machinist who will also advise on the correct type of jig to create. This would be an opportunity to build up a store of routed hulls to match your puttied bottles, whether you do it yourself or have the same skilled machinist do it for you.

My own machine set-up includes a MOTORISED FRETSAW used almost exclusively with coping-saw blades. Access to my wife's home-made LATHE (a 'Jackson special') made from an old washing-machine motor, enables me to turn lighthouses and other circular items.

Savings in time, however, should always be utilised in producing a better model than before – that's what it's all about. My criterion has always been – that if a machine will perform an operation as good as, or better than pure hand methods – then use it.

PHOTOGRAPH No. 30

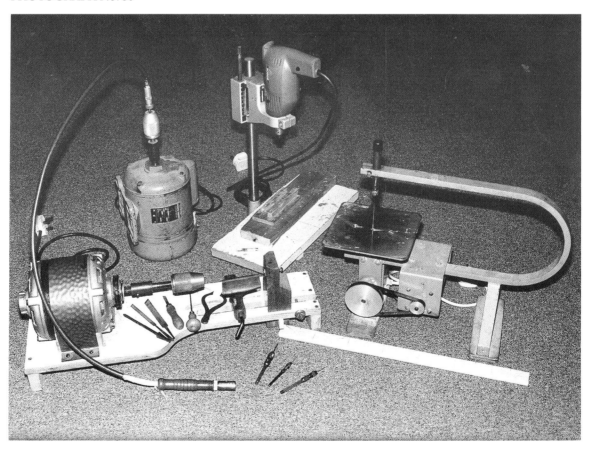

AN ARRANGEMENT OF USEFUL MACHINES

A PHOTOCOPIER with enlarging as well as reduction facility can prove extremely useful. My own up-to-date machine is capable of some extraordinary functions – in particular, the reducing or enlarging from one precise size to another. Take a plan of a ship with an overall length of, say, 220mm – it can be altered to any other given length by programming the original size, followed by the required one, by the mere pressing of a few buttons! The advantages are clearly obvious and, access to such a machine in Copy Shops is now quite commonplace.

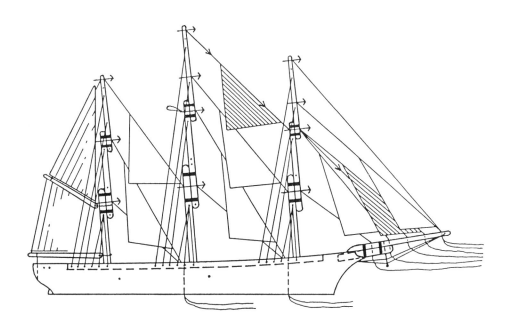

FIGURE 69

THICKNESS PLANER MACHINE: I never buy ready-to-use stripwood for hulls, pre-ferring instead to pay an occasional visit to the wood merchant of my choice – one who is invariably interested in my special requirements and always prepared to advise.

I take his small planks of wood to the local 'jobbing joiner' who first rough strips it on his circular saw then thickness-planes it precisely to whatever size is required. The speed of his operations and the negligible cost never ceases to amaze me.

71

CHAPTER 10

HINTS & TIPS

THE AUTHOR'S BOTTLE STAND is used mainly for demonstration purposes but the modeller could easily adapt this design for internal shelves with door front. If there is any tendency for movement at the bottle's base, double-sided sticky tape can be utilised to obviate this, as also on cradle stands.

If a PUTTY SEA has too much linseed oil content, vapour may emerge and cloud the bottle surface. Simply allow the sea longer to harden and then polish the glass. Old thin cotton handkerchiefs are ideal.

If the necessity arises to measure the INTERNAL HEIGHT OF A BOTTLE then this should be ascertained after puttying. Let the putty dry and then use a standard hull with an oversize central mast stepped to determine the overall useable space – a trial and error exercise. Hold the hull down in the groove with a 'manipulating' tool whilst drawing the mast erect.

I have sometimes seen internal as well as external diameter sizes moulded on a bottle's base. It's worth a look!

An easy way to establish LIGHTHOUSES inside bottles is to find 'rock material' into which a hole can be drilled to accept a glued in lighthouse. Manipulating the assemblage into a perfectly upright position inside the bottle is then much simpler – other rock pieces can be included, some with houses glued atop as required, to create an attractive scene.

REPETITIVE MESSAGES inside bottles can be photo copied and are indistinguishable from the purely handwritten article. 'Personalised' messages under the neck model can be written large and then reduced – there is no excuse for failing to record vital details about the ship, its creator, for whom the model was made and on what occasion!

PHOTOGRAPH No. 31

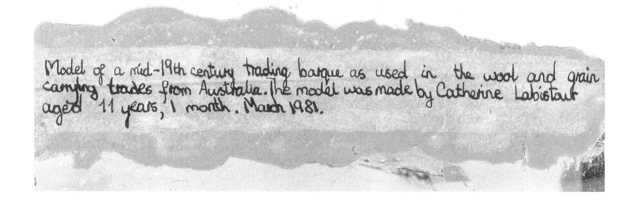

If you can cleverly MATCH THE COLOUR of the paper on which you write messages, to the putty, a quite startling effect can be achieved: the message appears to have been written on the glass itself, as the paper edges are not discernible. The effect is helped along if you use paper as fine as possible and cut the paper edge around the message in an irregular, wavy line.

Never pass up the opportunity to RECORD HISTORIC EVENTS on messages inside bottles. The value and interest of a SIB is greatly enhanced when it is so labelled. Shortly after the Falklands campaign, I was offered 800 standard 'Pusser's' rum bottles (all empty, of course), the contents of which had been decanted into traditional Royal Navy barrels, formerly used for the 'daily tot' ceremony – pre August 1970. Naturally, I accepted the offer, to my wife's chagrin, and we still have the majority of them – stored in every conceivable corner of the house. Each message, in circular format, is signed to give it a 'limited number' touch.

It tells of a job well done, after which the order was given to 'splice the mainbrace', although not strictly in the original sense as the free daily rum ration stopped 20 years ago.

Luck came my way on many similar occasions in the past – it's a long story! I will simply relate one that particularly appealed to me: a Whitby friend, retired antique dealer, rang me up a few years ago to say that he had just solved 'the mystery of the tea chests': He had bought a beautiful old farmstead on retiring, that required a certain amount of tidying up. In the corner of a barn were two tea chests – too heavy to move, and he promised himself to investigate them when time permitted. That day arrived and I was soon on my way to collect 42 superb Haig 'Dimple' bottles, generously given to me. They were all extremely dirty, and one contained the remains of the nest of an alcoholically minded field mouse! They cleaned easily to reveal superb quality glass – no tiresome embossed trade marks. This fact dated them as being quite old – a distinct acquisition for any SIB man.

The tip arising: when you use a MODERN 'DIMPLE' BOTTLE – always position the embossed 'Pinch' or 'Dimple' trade mark on the underside with the seam line opposite your viewing side.

A 'RUSE DE GUERRE' should always be neat. Make sure that the ends of your white bands around the hull are tapered (see Photo. No. 32). Mark in the dummy gunports with a sharp, hard pencil and then apply paint with a fine pen.

Some controversy exists as to the true origin of this popular form of hull decoration. It is said to originate from the days of piracy when a ship so painted could, from a distance, be mistaken for a vessel carrying guns and was, consequently, given a wide berth, hence the warlike connotation. Others declare this established custom to have resulted from the natural desire of ship owners to present their vessels in an attractive manner and to complement the beauty of the sail.

PHOTOGRAPH No. 32

MAILING MODELS – if you have occasion to send a model through the post – vibrations to which the bottle will be subjected may 'cockbill' yards. It is the author's routine to apply very small amounts of glue (as a final operation) to the points where lifts penetrate the masts on the port side – a tricky operation, possibly, but well worth it for the ease of mind afterwards. Begin with the aftermost mast first and make sure that yards are all correctly positioned immediately after glueing.

RATLINES are not so difficult to create and can all be put up 'in situ', although topmast ones involve advanced modelling. The author's method is to step each mast and rig out only the shrouds. A triangular template made from postcard and slightly wider than the shroud area is then neatly wedged between the shrouds and the mast. The card is nicked at appropriate intervals on each side. Then, with a fine knotted cotton threaded through a long needle, start at the bottom and pass the needle in front of and behind the template, securing in the nicks as you go. Try not to distort the shroudlines and work each side separately. Afterwards, glue where the lines touch – removing later with a new razor blade. The secret of success is in avoiding contact of the lines with the template when glueing up. Sewing needles prove useful in obviating that situation. Insert them horizontally twixt cottons and card where required. (Fig. 70).

If to be included, topmast shrouds with ratlines are best formed before the masts are stepped. Three shroud lines are sufficient and should pass through a drilled top – thence below to form futtock shrouds. Extra mast holes enable this operation to be carried out with one long continuous thread. A further tip: since holes drilled in a mast contribute to its susceptibility to breakage – always insert a small amount of glue on both sides of the mast, afterwards, where the lines penetrate.

A pair of templates is required to finish the job, as with care, it is possible to wrap on both port and starboard ratlines at the same time, with one continuous thread. (Fig. 71).

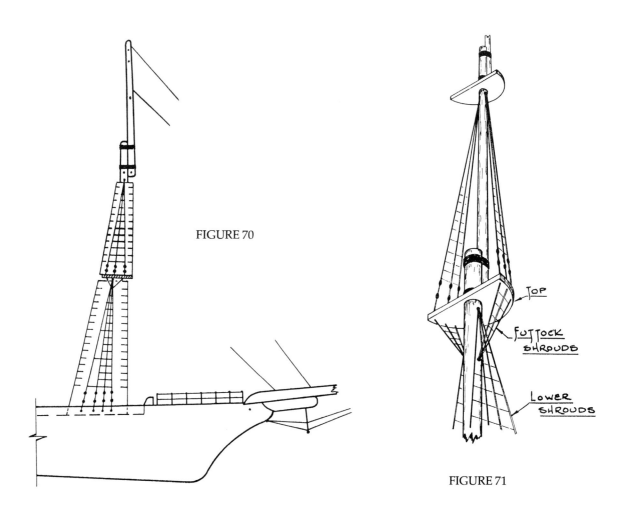

FIGURE 70

FIGURE 71

Difficulty in finding adequately strong cocktail sticks to use for masts was mentioned in Chapter 2. 'COTTON BUDS', available from most chemists, are sometimes constructed from fine quality dowel, and quite usable. It would be wise, however, to discover if the particular manufacturer has 'gone plastic' – before buying.

SHROUDS AND BACKSTAYS – strictly speaking, should normally sit inside the bulwarks of a sailing ship. Of necessity, however, modellers in many instances resort to some form of compromise and where lines contrast against the bulwark, they can be well disguised by 'painting out' with the same colour used behind them.

FOR AUTHENTICITY – the experienced modeller who wishes to put his lines inboard should drill the bulwark as near the capping as he dares rather than at deck level. The effect (see Fig. 72) is greatly to be desired. This is work for the careful, more adventurous modeller who would do well to glue every line as it passes through its respective hole in the bulwark, thereby ensuring maximum security from breakage of the delicate capping.

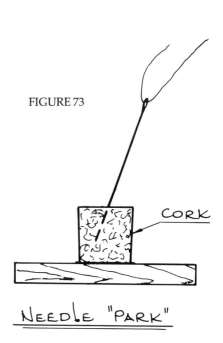

FIGURE 73

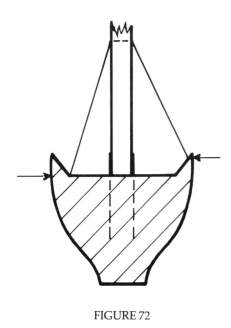

FIGURE 72

NEEDLE "PARK"

No. 10 sewing needles that the Author uses exclusively for rigging models are about the finest on general sale. They are, to say the least, – elusive; drop one and you can search for ages until you find it. It's a good habit to keep only one in use at a time – and endeavour to have it always cotton-threaded. A threaded needle is always easier to find whether on the floor somewhere, stuck in your jumper, or hiding amongst your worktable clutter! A good tip is to glue a cork to a piece of wood and PARK YOUR NEEDLE safely when not in use – even momentarily. (Fig. 73).

Two HALF HULLS for the price of one results from the following tip: when making adapted 'Collector's' model, for instance, in Chapter 7: – you should carefully prepare two identical pieces of wood 3/4" x 7/16" x 7¼" with two of the wide faces really smooth and clean. These sides will be glued together, separated by a piece of newspaper 1" x 11/16" x 7½" i.e. an overlap of 1/8" all round. Glue the sides to be joined and rub them together to achieve overall evenness and then interpose the paper. Endeavour to coincide the pieces of wood perfectly together – gently clamped in a vice afterwards. When set, you proceed to make up a Collector's hull in the normal way. On completion, the two halves are separated by prising, at the stern end, into the joint with a fine, blunt knife.
If it resists, 'humour the grain' by prising at the bow.
Follow through along the entire length slowly and carefully.

Simple NECK MODEL HULLS in various sizes are easily made using standard dowels. Take a 10″ length of 1/4″ dowel – mark it off into hull lengths and carve out the sheer from both hulls on the ends. (Fig. 74).

The same basic hull can be used for a sailing cutter or a tug boat, but for the latter, create a blunt, 'bluff' profile.

FIGURE 74

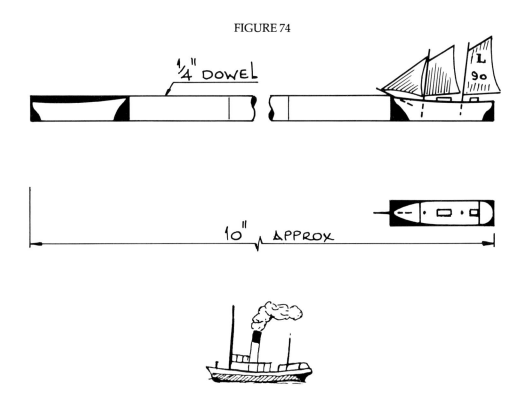

Next carve out the two sterns and sand to shape. Carving and sanding in the length comes much easier, as does the drilling. Prick 'pilotholes' where you wish to position masts and then drill with an appropriate size to take a monofilament which, incidentally, you can find on all manner of household articles e.g. yard, clothes and scrubbing brushes. Drill at a raked-back angle for effect. Now saw off the two hulls, shape and sand the bows. A drilled hole will be required for the bowsprit and you will probably have to create a sanded 'flat' on which to prick a pilot hole. Usable height in bottle necks will vary tremendously – ascertain yours before making and glueing sails in position. The masts will spring up readily after insertion in the bottle.

A point was made in Chapter 4 (extra rigging) that the individual modeller must make up his own mind where to draw the line as to added detail. Experimentation is the best way to find out, if doubt arises. Delicacy of detail at this stage, however, is always called for and there are many books available to help in deciding what to add next to enhance effect.

On those occasions when the author was not available to demonstrate in the Exhibition Centre, it was a distinct advantage to have created a VIDEO FILM. This shows the making of a 'Collector's' model and the bottling process. From this exercise emerged a useful tip – although of use only to the experienced modeller who, like myself, is interested in pursuing the antique look. It was decided to do a complete 'dummy run' first, which involved 1. bottling and erection in the bottle 2, collapsing the tophamper and retrieval from the bottle. This went smoothly and proved that the filming could proceed without problem.

Having tidied the entire ship, I was quite struck to discover a most enhanced appearance in the sails due, of course, to the crushing in the bottle neck and subsequent manipulation back to shape. It is now a matter of routine to repeat this performance on all models. After all, the maximum time taken on a 'Collectors' model amounts to no more than 5 minutes.

Some people find it useful to IDENTIFY LINES that emerge out of the bottle neck. My suggestion is that you could paint the last inch of each cotton a different colour, keeping the same sequence on all models from bowsprit end through to the hull lines.

Whenever confronted by AWKWARD SHAPED BOTTLES (e.g. the 'House of Lords') it is routine for the author to remove all bowsprit lines before 'bedding' the ship. This obviates making an elaborate severing tool and is simply a case of following the same routine in Chapter 5 under 'Securing and removal of Bowsprit lines'.

BUNT LINES, LEECH LINES, and REEF BANDS on sails, whether simulated by pencilling on – or fashioned from cotton and glued in position, is a case in point. On a ship, these lines are employed in gathering up sails when furling. A sail is secured in position with reef points on both sides of the sail, thereby reducing sail area in adverse conditions. In addition BRAILS on spanker sails, used for the same purpose, can look quite effective. Do seek out additional reading that will show you the variations, one sail from the next. (Fig. 75).

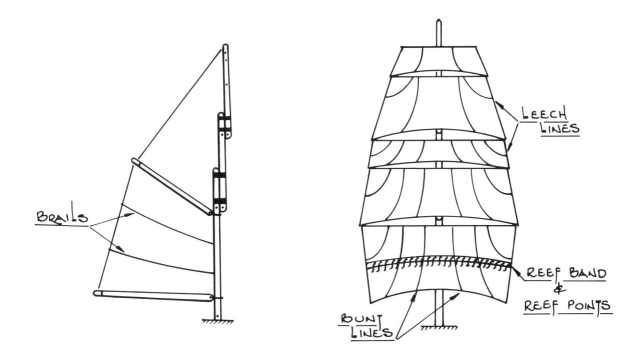

FIGURE 75

CHAPTER 11

CONCLUSION

I WOULD venture to say now, in this concluding chapter, that the modeller who has followed my guidelines throughout – acting on all the various techniques – has, potentially at his fingertips, a craft second to none. Furthermore, it is one requiring a negligible financial outlay – compared with some; needs little work space – it can be carried out on a corner of the kitchen table or on a tray by the fireside; with a little discipline – is clean; and given a reasonable standard – produces a readily saleable end product, if that is of any consideration.

An earlier observation made in the book stresses the eventual scope for inventiveness and artistic skills. This is where the real interest begins and, to my mind, what it's all about. Whichever craft a modeller opts to pursue, complete satisfaction is guaranteed when individuality is allowed to assert itself. Indeed, you may allow the mind to run riot – and why not? As the Japanese gentleman did, for example, who produced a beautiful period ship within a 'standard' bottle – a type motivated by banks of oars during windless conditions. Construction apart, (and this ship had to pass through the neck and be assembled piecemeal within the bottle) what a startling revelation, on completion, to see the entire complement of oars moving in rhythm on both sides of the vessel, at the flick of a switch. No wonder he was heard to remark that "to create this one it was necessary to work double in hardship!" Congratulations are certainly in order to this modeller for introducing a further, acceptable, dimension to our craft.

Ship in bottle making can be a very sociable pursuit. By its very nature, the subject invites and makes conversation, particularly when a complex model such as the foregoing is under discussion. Throughout the entire world, makers, collectors and enthusiasts generally have been forming Associations over the past two decades – their Membership ever increasing. It has been another revelation for each and every person to discover, not only how prevalent is the Craft, but the amazing standards achieved by some modellers.

Illustrating a few points already made, let me relate one of many interesting episodes from the past:–

When our small family 'wintered out' England's three worst months in sunnier places as a matter of routine each new year, the South of France was our chosen venue, initially, until we discovered the better climate and delights of Southern Spain. Wherever we found ourselves, it was no problem settling down to income producing work – indeed, away from the exigencies of home routine and into a relaxed atmosphere, most of our production was in S.I.B's, which sold easily and financed the entire trip, with something left over!

On one of the early trips, we were motoring homeward bound, up through Germany to take the ferry at Rotterdam. We stayed overnight at an hotel in Heidelberg, a particularly nice one, and were presented with our bill after breakfast – no problem, except that the hotel proprietor would not accept a Travellers cheque. Britain had, at that precise point in time, devalued the pound and no-one had any idea as to the new exchange rate. We could find no-one who would handle our travellers' cheques – this was Britain's second devaluation in a fairly short space of time. Suspicion lurked!

Meanwhile, the hotel bill in precise Deutschmark/Pfennigs figures, leered eloquently and menacingly at us. It was time for action – decisive and quick, as we had 'deadlines' to make.

I had a habit in those days of making up a 'special model' in amongst the 'pot-boilers' – to keep my sanity, I always said! On this trip, I got carried away with one such 'collector's piece' and it had turned out magnificently, the best thing I had ever made. It was certainly not my intention ever to sell it. But, needs must and I determined to part with it for the precise amount of the bill.

Leaving the family behind, I sped into town taking the model and scoured around for a likely antique shop – (they were always first and best choice). As luck would have it, the first one I happened upon had a high shelf running around the whole shop with ships in bottles, nose to tail, filling it! At a glance, I could see that they were all of recent manufacture and very poor quality. My hopes rose! The proprietor, an extraordinary character with nautical interest, took one look at my model and exclaimed "I **must** have! How much, please?" I don't remember, of course, the amount of the hotel bill, but in these days, I might well have been saying, for example, "297DM.17". "I pay, I pay . . . . . . but please tell me why you ask for such an unusual amount?" After the explanation and a brief account of our 'working holiday', he telephoned the hotel and then made out his cheque for the agreed amount.

With the model in his hands, he thereupon made a statement which, for me, was a cause for some disappointment a few years later: he said "My grandchildren already have this model!" and then insisted that before our family left Heidelberg, we must write up all the background story about ourselves as a document to go with his purchase. This my wife did quickly, carefully, and attractively on 'antiqued' paper – and we left behind a delighted customer ('Tiger' he said everyone called him!)

It was only a few years later when, one day, a young American couple called at our shop in Robin Hood's Bay, established my identity, and then produced the papers Pat had written. My initial disappointment was quelled completely when I learned that their England trip was based on finding the creator of the model which 'Tiger' had parted with. It was, they said, their pride and joy and had been established in a recess specially chipped out of the stone fireplace in their living room. For me, the joy was in knowing that my 'Collector's Piece' now really did have a **permanent** home.

Commissions of models for famous people or to mark special occasions are always welcomed as one tends to tire (I'm sure most people do) of 'run of the mill' activity from time to time. In this respect, I enjoyed one particular commission by the Coal Factors Society in London to commemorate the closing down of their Tilbury signal station after 200 years continuous operation. This involved making upwards of some 70 four masted barques in old style 70cl Teacher whisky bottles, each with a general text under the main model, naming the recipient and the number of years service given to the firm. Sir Derek Ezra was one of these, and his precise connection was duly noted.

The neck of the bottle carried a minute signal station designed from photographs and you will understand the relief one feels to have a partner, at times such as this, who can 'pitch in' and get the work done. My 'First Mate' has a propensity for creating really small objects and was here in her element, first designing and then making.

So much does she enjoy really small work, it was always taken as read that she would make all figureheads on Collectors models and two appropriate 'one-offs' that turned out really impressively were for prominent people in different walks of life. First of these models was for Admiral of the Fleet Sir Terence Lewin to commemorate his appointment to the Board of Trustees of the National Maritime Museum. The figurehead depicted an Admiral saluting! It was commissioned by Charles Tobias, Vice-President of the Museum's 'Friends Association' and proprietor of Pussers Rum Ltd, a firm he founded to compensate for the break in R.N. tradition (Aug. 1st, 1970) when the daily tot was terminated; a good portion of the profits from sale of this British Navy Pussers Rum is passed on to naval charities. The back of this book cover displays a collier brig (the 'Richard') in a standard Pussers bottle.

Second of the 'Mate's' impressive figureheads fronted a ship in bottle specially commissioned as a gift for a world famous orchestral conductor.

When 'personalising' features were being discussed, her brief was a rather challenging one – the figure had to be an actual representation of the conductor himself with arms outstretched holding a tiny baton, a wide expanse of shirt cuff showing – a feature for which he was, in fact, well known. Additionally, the underlying text was required in Czechoslovakian but this presented no problem – merely a careful copying job. Needless to say, Pat rose to the occasion and the recipient was highly delighted.

"How did you actually get started?" is a question constantly directed at me from the many people I meet – the cryptic and true answer "By being born the second son" only forthcoming when I have time to relate the circumstances . . . . . I was born second son in a family of six children. Our father, a Mauritian-born Master Mariner, met mother (a Cambridge lass) in London and when they married, settled for a family home in Hull into which port Dad often docked and where he had very good friends including a fellow lay-preacher and his wife. Dad's early and untimely death at sea when all the children were still at school or, as yet, unborn like the third son, caused a family crisis which had to be overcome. 'Auntie and Uncle', from that point, were particularly supportive and always gave the family whatever help they could. My elder brother and I had our dinner with them each school day for quite some time which afforded much relief for our mother, especially on Mondays – wash day!

I don't think we missed out on one occasion to sit down and admire a ship in bottle made by our Dad, and to envy their possession of it . . . . It was a four masted barque anchored in harbour with dock buildings for background – how we loved it and coveted it. We didn't have one at home!!

PHOTOGRAPH No. 33

Model by the Author's Father

It was also our great delight to hear from Uncle Charles, the story behind the creation of Dad's model: "Sitting around the fire one day, your father took a stick of firewood from the hearth, opened out his penknife and whittled away the ship's hull. He used spent matches for the masts and spars, needles and thread from Auntie's workbox – in fact, we found everything necessary around the house to make that beautiful four masted barque with its painted background". Everything, I should say – with the exception of the empty Teacher Whisky bottle (being the home of a Temperance Lay preacher!). As the years rolled by, our fascination never wavered and then it was revealed that "On our death, Louis (the eldest) would inherit the SIB and Léon the large painting of SS 'Moorby'" (one of Dad's ships) that hung over the fireplace. Although a superb painting, I could not conceal my disappointment. Thus it was, and soon after, I softened the blow by seeking out a Hobby shop kit and set about the task of making my own. It was quite a complex model – a three masted Clipper ship with 26 sails set but I completed it fairly easily, and then looked to the bottling. What a job – I finished up literally on my knees at the kitchen table, encountering every kind of pitfall – finally declaring this to be 'the first and last'! Still seeking to emulate Dad, however, I then started to design my own – going on better with each succeeding model and finding myself firmly 'hooked'. You know what I mean!

When I opened my Hull Arts and Crafts shop years later, having forsaken an office desk, the odd SIB sale came in quite useful. My story is now developing into 'How I carried on'. Well, to cut a long story short – I tested the mail order market through the well known 'Sea Breezes' magazine. The response was quite remarkable, orders regularly coming from world wide. A pen friendship developed with a young American who persuaded me to advertise in 'Skipper', a U.S. publication which carried my ad. for years until becoming defunct, the only payment being 'in kind' – an occasional SIB.

Days after the first ad. broke, my doormat was awash with mail and continued for quite some time. Outstanding orders often developed, because of other commitments, to embarassing proportions – but I fought on manfully, alone!

How the sun and stars have shone for me at times, for into my life came, just then, 'she who now must be obeyed' bringing not only her delightful self, a firm grasp upon a multiplicity of skills and talents . . . . . but (believe it or not), a lifelong curiosity about the SIB 'mystery'. Her first-class needle working expertise reduced complex ship rigging to childsplay!

I am often asked what one has to do to to achieve a varied and interesting lifestyle such as I enjoy. There are many factors involved. Paramount amongst these, is to acquire a wife/working partner with temperament and abilities such as mine possesses. This is an extremely rare species, however.

You could spend a lifetime looking for one!!

GLOSSARY
GLOSSARY OF TERMS USED IN THE BOOK

AFT – at the stern. Behind.

BACKSTAYS – ropes running aft of the masts to the bulwarks to impart lateral stability and providing additional support to the shrouds.

BARQUE – a sailing ship of three or more masts, all square rigged except the aftermost, which is rigged fore-and-aft.

BINNACLE – a wooden compass-housing standing on deck by the wheel.

BOLLARD – vertical pieces of timber or iron fixed on deck, to which ropes are made fast.

BOOM – the lower spar fixed to the mizzen or jigger mast, carrying the spanker sail.

BOWSPRIT – a projecting spar from the fo'c'sle head, on top of which is fixed a longer one (the jibboom).

BOWSPRIT SHROUDS – an arrangement of wire ropes from each stem of a ship to the bowsprit for support.

BOW – the foremost end of a ship, opposite to stern.

BLOCK – a wooden case with interior turning sheave through which ropes are inserted to increase mechanical power applied to them.

BRACES – a rope used for trimming a yard relative to wind direction.

BRAILS – ropes on either side of a spanker sail used for gathering it in to the mast when furling.

BULWARK – raised woodwork along the sides of a ship above her upper decks.

BUNT LINES – ropes leading from the foot of a sail for taking it in or reefing.

CAPPING – a strip of wood fitted to the top of the bulwarks.

CAPSTAN – an upright cylindrical barrel fitted on deck and used for winding chain or ropes. Operated either by steam or manually with capstan bars.

COCK BILLED – a yard across a mast at an angle, sometimes deliberately trimmed thus as an indication of mourning.

CUTWATER – a curved timber fixed to the stem of a ship for protection and sometimes known as the knee or beakhead.

DAVITS – crane-like devices from which lifeboats are hung. Older types twised in sockets at the base to swing boats inboard if required.

DOLPHIN STRIKER – a short perpendicular spar under the bowsprit used for holding down the jibboom.

DOUBLING – portions which overlap on a mast made up of two or more joined spars.

FIGURE HEAD – the decorative carved figure set below the bowsprit of a ship, usually representing some aspect of the ship's name or function.

FORE/AFT – (as to direction) – from the stern of a ship looking forward to the bows.

FORECASTLE (FO'C'SLE) – spar beneath the raised deck forward, used as living quarters for the crew.

FUTTOCK SHROUDS – a kind of short shroud set under the top on a lower mast to give support, and is perhaps a seaman's corruption of 'foot hook'.

GAFF – the upper spar carrying the spanker sail.

HATCH – an opening in the ship's deck for loading and unloading cargo, possibly also giving access to people to decks below.

HULL – the main body of a ship i.e. upper deck, sides and bottom only.

JIBBOOM – see bowsprit.

JIBSAILS – triangular sails set by sailing vessels on the foremast stays.

LEECH LINES – ropes leading from the leeches (the sides of a sail) used for gathering in when furling.

LIFT – wire ropes or chains supporting yards from the masthead.

POOP – a raised deck at the aftermost part of a ship.

PORT – left hand side of a ship as seen from the stern looking forward.

PORTHOLE – circular hole on a ships side cut out to admit light and air. The correct more seamanlike term should really be "scuttle".

RAKE – (of a mast) the angle, relative to the perpendicular, in a fore-aft direction.

RATLINES – short length of rope seized across the shrouds to form a ladder and provide access aloft.

REEF BAND – a strip of canvas across a sail which gives extra strength at the reef points.

REEF POINTS – short lengths of rope set in the reef bands of a sail used to tie down a reef (shorten sail).

RUNNING RIGGING – rigging for hoisting and generally manipulating sails and yards of a ship.

RUSE DE GUERRE – a striking form of hull decoration representing dummy gun ports on a wide band.

SHEER – the upward curve of the deck of a ship towards bows and stern.

SHIP-RIGGED – a vessel with square sails set on all masts.

SHIP SHAPE – in good and seamanlike condition. The full expression is 'shipshape and Bristol fashion', originating from the days when Bristol was the major west coast port and all its shipping was kept in very good order.

SHROUDS – rigging on a sailing ship used to impart lateral stability to masts.

SPANKER – a large fore-and-aft sail set between the gaff and boom.

SPAR – in general, masts, yards, gaffs, booms, etc. used as supports in the rigging of a ship.

SQUARE SAILS – sails fixed on yards set across the ship, i.e. square rigged.

STANCHIONS – upright supports on the deck side which carry a guardrail.

STANDING RIGGING – fixed, permanent rigging of a ship.

STARBOARD – the right side of a ship from the stern looking for'ard.

STAYS – ropes used to brace masts in for-and-aft direction.

STAYSAILS – sails attached to stays in a fore-and-aft direction.

STERN – the after end of a ship.

TOP – a platform set at the mast doublings on a sailing ship which is mainly utilised to extend topmast shrouds which give additional support to the topmast.

TOPHAMPER – all masts, yards, rigging, etc. atop the deck.

TOPMAST – in sailing vessels, that mast next above the lower mast.

WETTED AREA – (of a hull) that part of the hull of a ship in contact with the water. When sailing, the smaller the contact – the greater the speed (and vice versa).

YARD – a spar crossed either horizontally or diagonally on a mast from which a sail is set.

YARD-ARM – the ends of a yard outside the lifts.

INDEX

OWN NOTES

OWN NOTES

OWN NOTES

OWN NOTES

OWN NOTES